The Regulation School: A Critical Introduction

Robert Boyer

The Regulation School:
A Critical Introduction

TRANSLATED BY CRAIG CHARNEY

Columbia University Press   New York

COLUMBIA UNIVERSITY PRESS

NEW YORK   OXFORD

Library of Congress Cataloging-in-Publication Data

Boyer, Robert.
  [Théorie de la régulation. English]
  The regulation school : a critical introduction / Robert Boyer ;
translated by Craig Charney.
      p.   cm.
  Translation of: La théorie de la régulation.
  Bibliography: p.
  Includes index.
  ISBN 0-231-06548-5
  1. France—Economic Policy—1981–   2. Equilibrium (Economics)
I. Title.
HC276.3.B6913   1989
338.944′009′048—dc20   89-7221
                              CIP

Casebound editions of Columbia University Press books are Smyth-sewn and
printed on permanent and durable acid-free paper

Printed in the United States of America

c 10 9 8 7 6 5 4 3 2 1

Contents

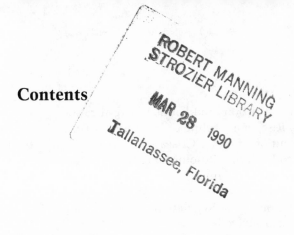

Contents

Introduction to the English-Language Edition

Why is the current economic crisis not just a repetition of that of 1929, despite the fears reawakened by the crash of 1987? How can we explain why the rapid growth of the postwar years led to a period of uncertainty in the 1970s, in which the principal economic indicators deteriorated? Had the developed capitalist economies overcome these difficulties by the end of the 1980s? Finally, what could account for the sharply contrasting strategies and patterns of development of the United States, South East Asia, and Europe over these years? The national and historical forms taken by economic growth and crisis make up the central questions explored by the regulation approach. This book offers an overview of the research conducted on these themes over more than a decade, presenting its strengths, weaknesses, and potential. At the outset essentially a French product, and later a European one, this work has begun to attract some attention in both North and South America. The considerable interest evoked by the first international conference on regulation theory, held in Barcelona in June 1988, provided evidence of this.

Steadily developing since the 1970s, theories of regulation bring together elements from several social scientific traditions. They begin with a critique of orthodox Marxism, since they reject the idea of general, eternal laws applicable to all socioeconomic systems. Instead, they draw upon the contributions of structuralism, which offered new foundations for concepts such as relations of production, modes of production, etc. However, regulation theorists recognize that a given social relation can taken on different historical forms, which help shape the configuration of social classes and the dynamics of the economy. Since they take the historical character of capitalism seriously, researchers using these approaches find the work of the *Annales* school to be another source of inspiration. Reacting against the rather fossilized Marxism of the interwar years, its founding fathers showed how the dynamics of both business cycles and major crises depend upon the forms of productive structures and social relations.

On these foundations were developed the key concepts of regulation theory: institutional forms, the wage relation, regimes of accumulation, and modes of regulation—their combination defining a mode of development. When tested against the history of the United States and the major countries of Europe, and of some Latin American countries as well, this construct has provided elements of a response to the three questions with which this preface opened. If the crash of 1987 did not lead rapidly to the depression many expected, it is because America's contemporary mode of development is not the same as during the interwar years. The sequence of events in the two crises has thus been completely different, as are the interconnections beween the spheres of finance and accumulation. Likewise, the advanced capitalist countries have not followed identical strategies in their search for a new mode of development. Their particular social compromises, unequal degrees of acceptance of the new production methods, and sometimes opposed economic policy choices lie behind the distinctly unequal macroeconomic performances of the United States, Japan, and Europe. Finally, the causes and course of the crisis were present in outline within the previous mode of development. As time passed, its contradictions and disequilibria could no longer be contained by the workings of the existing institutional forms and mode of regulation. Yesterday's strengths have become today's weaknesses and vice versa, although there is no general law at work in the matter. This, in a nutshell, is the point of regulation theory, for which the present work is intended to make a case.

That being said, this introduction is intended to update the discussion of certain questions dealt with in the 1986 French edition, to spell out the regulation school's views on the dynamics of American capitalism, and to explore its relationship to some recent work by the American school of radical political economy. One of the first works to present a regulation theory analysis to the American public was that of Michel Aglietta (1982). Then came various works by Alain Lipietz (1985, 1987). Nor should we forget the general presentation of the theory by Michel de Vroey (1984). Not surprisingly, the conclusions of these authors have been under continuous fire from economic theorists and from specialists in American history. To begin with, therefore, we propose to respond to some of their principal objections.

FORDISM: A CENTRAL YET MISUNDERSTOOD CONCEPT

A conclusion on which a number of studies based upon the regulation approach have agreed is that the rapid growth of the postwar era can be attributed to a novel regime of accumulation: Fordism. Under this regime the development of the means of production sector of the economy went together with the modernization of the consumer goods sector, whose expansion was stimulated by an apparently unprecedented labor-capital compromise. The task of management was to remodel the labor process according to the canons of scientific management, while the concern of unions was to ensure that workers benefited from the corresponding productivity increases, through strikes or negotiations. This hypothesis, which suggests a certain number of historical inquiries or sociological studies, has given rise to several misunderstandings. Let us try to clear up some of them.

To give the name of Detroit's celebrated automaker to a regime of accumulation, a Marxist concept if there is one, may seem paradoxical, indeed, unnatural. The historians who have examined Ford's high-wage policy in the 1920s have concluded that it was essentially a strategy for limiting labor turnover, by creating a significant wage gap compared to alternative jobs. Those who hold to the concept of "efficient wages" could even see it as telling historical evidence in favor of the hypothesis that high wages are a way to control the intensity of work and to stimulate worker effort. Gramsci, who was the first to suggest the notion of Fordism, emphasized the role that a high-wage policy could play in improving workers' "morality" and social integration.[1] In his view, Ford's key objectives were combating alcoholism (with its damaging consequences for industrial efficiency) and stabilizing working-class families.

In short, it would be an illusion to take the American industrialist's claims at face value when he argued that the workers would

1. *Translator's note:* See "Americanism and Fordism," in Antonio Gramsci, *Selections from the Prison Notebooks* (New York: International Publishers, 1971).

become consumers of the very products they had helped make. How-ever, his personal aims do not affect the concept of Fordism, which is intended to characterize the macroeconomic conditions governing accumulation. The preceding objections only illustrate the complex-ity involved in moving from the level of the firm—even a large one—to that of the whole economy. If, in fact, only the modern sectors of industry had established higher wages, the new model of consumption could not have been generalized across the whole of the work force and become a norm conforming to the imperatives of mass production itself. Certainly, the extraordinary decline in the relative price of the Model T Ford allowed it to be bought by many, including workers. However, Fordism, as a regime of accumulation, supposes a relative homogenization of wage increases irrespective of the status and skill level of workers, not just high wages in Detroit.

Consequently, the modernizing employers' initiatives required a complimentary set of institutions which established relative uni-formity in wage increases. In the United States, the effects of collec-tive bargaining were extended by "connective bargaining," which, starting from the auto industry, propagated increases in incomes to the nonunionized private sector, then to the public sector. Such a mechanism is the condition of a simultaneous evolution of the norms of production and consumption. A Fordist innovator therefore does not suffice to establish Fordism. Historical research on the French firm Renault (Ford's French equivalent, proportionately speaking) clearly shows the lag which can develop between advances at the microeconomic level and institutional forms and modes of regulation. Between the world wars, trade union struggles at Renault led to a contract which in principle guaranteed workers the near-indexation of wages to prices and a share in productivity gains. But since the agreement was limited to Renault, the firm suffered a competitive disadvantage and lost market share, eliminating the workers' strong bargaining position. Only in the postwar era would Renault play a determining role in the setting of the average wage level. Then, the dynamic growth of production would be matched by a roughly equivalent increase in real wages, leading to rises in con-sumption and investment as wage labor became the predominant form of economic activity. In other words, Fordism only makes sense at the level of the whole economy, even if this does some violence to the image conveyed by the reference to the industrial pioneer from Detroit.

TECHNICAL CONTINUITY VERSUS CHANGE IN THE MODE OF REGULATION

A second major objection to the concept of Fordism holds that it suggests a debatable discontinuity in a process of technological evolution marked by the spread of the "American system," which was unlike English-style manufacturing. In the American case, it is difficult to distinguish a phase of intensive accumulation from another, more extensive, regime solely through changes in the organization of industrial labor. Morever, data on labor productivity trends, like those concerning overall factors output, reveal more continuities than breakpoints, even if the latter are not entirely absent in periods such as the 1920s.

In this respect, the economic history of the United States is indeed perceptibly different from that of the European countries or Japan. The latters' adoption of the "American way of life" after 1945 led them to catch up with the production and consumption norms of North America. Consequently, the breakpoint in productivity trends is marked in these countries, and can easily be observed in a statistical analysis. Nevertheless, the hypothesis of a transition to Fordism should not be rejected for the United States. To begin with, histories of the labor process, such as Hounshell (1984), show noteworthy reorganizations, particularly in the 1920s and 1930s. From one decade to the next, the lesser or greater vigor of the accumulation process explains the changes in the productivity growth rate. Moreover, the macroeconomic time series for the postwar era reveal an attenuation of the depth and duration of the traditional business cycle, an indication of a change in the mode of regulation.

Finally, more theoretically oriented work aimed at formalizing the various regimes of accumulation has shown that the same mode of production organization can be combined with different regimes of demand, leading to differing long-term economic dynamics (Boyer 1988). In these conditions, technical continuity or gradual change is not necessarily incompatible with discontinuity in the mode of regulation. On this point, the regulation approach resembles catastrophe theory in mathematics. In nonlinear dynamic systems—even simple ones—a control variable which changes in a regular manner can produce the discontinuous evolution of dependent variables. The hypothesis of Fordism thus merits consideration for the United States, even if the empirical evidence initially suggested by Aglietta requires reexamination in the light of more recent historical work and long-term macroeconomic time series. Let us hope that the publication of this book helps stimulate such research.

A REGIME OF ACCUMULATION IS MORE THAN A PRODUCTION PROCESS

A third methodological criticism points to the ambiguity of the concept of Fordism regarding the passage from the micro level to the macro level. For purposes of popularization, some presentations of the regulation approach have made use of two questionable simplifications. On the one hand, the labor process is treated as though it were the beginning and end of the regime of accumulation, obscuring its other determinants. This has resulted in the tendency to infer the likely existence of a Fordist mode of development, perhaps somewhat modified, from the utilization of Fordist techniques in certain sectors or firms. On the other hand, the relevance of the concept of Fordism can be challenged on the grounds that none of the dominant firms in some sectors conformed to its canons of workplace organization.

Concerning the first point, production relations—in this instance, the wage relation—have been shown to play a determining role in the process by which regimes of accumulation succeed each other. But it would be a mistake to analyze the wage relation solely on the basis of the labor process. It is perfectly possible for a mass production system, utilizing mechanized assembly lines, to exist without long-term contracts governing the wage relation, an essential characteristic of Fordism. It is for this reason that concepts such as "bloody Taylorism" or "peripheral Fordism" are more dangerous than fruitful. Just because Ford builds cars in Brazil, does that allow the establishment of parallels between the Brazilian and American regimes of accumulation? A closer look will lead, on the contrary, to the characterization of the mode of development of the newly industrialized countries as quite distinctive. Moreover, such claims of parallels do not take into account that the time horizons involved in investment decisions, as well as the associated forms of competition and monetary regime, all constitute essential elements of the mode of regulation associated with Fordism.

Studies of individual firms, for their part, have revealed the complexity of the mediations through which the effects of a dominant form of production organization are felt at the macroeconomic level. It would have been convenient to imagine that Fordism was an economy-wide extrapolation of the large-scale auto producer. In fact, understanding the relationship between these two levels of observation requires more rigorous analysis. As we have seen, a few modern-style firms may not be enough to bring about the establishment of a Fordist regime of accumulation. Moreover, this regime does not always have assembly-line consumer durables production as its basis. A final paradox is that the very success of Fordist methods in manufacturing can be associated with the growth of sectors operating according to an almost entirely different logic, the construction and service sectors offering striking examples.

In effect, Fordism should be thought of as an ideal type, whose logic operates at the level of the accumulation process taken as a whole, not as the exclusive principle organizing all production. The mode of regulation, in turn, involves all the sectoral and national peculiarities which explain the adjustment process that connects production and social demand.

The Crisis of Fordism: Mirage or Reality?

If one admits that the concept of Fordism helps us describe an important aspect of contemporary capitalist economies, does it provide a useful characterization of the current crisis? A number of objections have been raised on this score by Brenner (1988), Bernstein (1988), and Dumenil and Levy (1988), along with many other participants in the Barcelona conference. Why, they have asked, have slowdowns in growth and recessions been simultaneous, when Fordism is at unequal stages of development in different countries? Is it possible to explain a sharp shift in growth trends through the slow exhaustion of productivity potential? What is the empirical evidence regarding the economic and social limits of the postwar regime of accumulation? All these questions have not been finally resolved, but important recent advances have been achieved recently regarding them.

Essentially, the remarkable synchronization of short-term economic dynamics observable since the 1960s reflects the increasingly international character of the accumulation process. If the slowdown in productivity growth and the decline of profit rates first appeared in the United States in the late 1960s, inflationary pressures, the manifestation of the creeping crisis, were transmitted to other countries, threatening the stability of the international monetary system. Contracyclical policies inspired by Keynesianism were undermined by these developments, to the point where they lost a large part of their effectiveness. From this point on, two crises were superimposed, one upon the other. One, slow in developing and somewhat hidden, concerned the very principles governing accumulation. The other, much more rapid and visible, involved the principal linkages between inflation, employment, and budgetary and trade imbalances. Nonetheless, these two aspects of the crisis were not unrelated. Is it not part of the logic of the Fordist model to seek economies of scale through the rapid expansion first of domestic markets, then of markets abroad? Because of this fact, national growth regimes have shifted from complimentarity to competition since World War II, so that the semi-automatic stabilizing properties of the international economic system have been compromised. Thus, in a more complete analysis, the two causes of the crisis can be linked to each other, and tied to the Fordist regime of accumulation. Naturally, in each nation-state, the nature of the processes by which money is created, the country's international position, and its economic policy must be taken into account, not just the dialectical relation between production and consumption norms.

Once this is recognized, it can explain the apparent paradox of sharp changes within a mode of development whose structural characteristics are only slowly affected by the contradictions to which it gives rise. It is true, in fact, that simulations conducted with sectoral models dealing with France (Bertrand 1983) and the United States (Juillard 1988) have found a tendency toward slower growth, rather than the marked short-run changes observed after the oil shocks and countershocks. It thus becomes necessary to call in explanatory factors in addition to the regime of accumulation in the strict sense of the term. These include changes in the terms of trade between raw materials and energy and manufactured goods; the reordering of the international division of manufacturing production; and the slow decay of some of the bases of American hegemony for want of its expression in monetary terms, the dollar being the pivot of the international monetary system. However, in a fuller analysis of the problem, it would be possible to include factors which initially appear exogenous. The international division of labor, far from being outside the scope of Fordism, became its very expression, to the point where it gave rise to new disequilibria.

Such is undoubtedly one of the most promising paths for research, which Lipietz and Mistral have already begun to explore. It is true that our understanding of international regimes must be considerably improved if we are to have a solid foundation for the development of regulation theory in this area. The developments of the 1980s show clearly the need for this. The dominant countries have continued to set their economic policies with domestic objectives as their top priority, even if they are constrained by the international economic situation. For instance, England and West Germany have been preoccupied by the risks of resurgent inflation, while the United States has struggled to reduce its foreign deficits. The combination of such policies at the international level can accentuate the instability which has marked trade patterns, through a series of interest rate increases, for instance. In the dialectic between the national and the international, research on regulation has long tended to focus on the former. Now it is important for such work to explore the latter. This, moreover, is the direction taken by the recent work of Aglietta (1986), whose role in the launching of the regulation school has been mentioned.

As to the empirical proof of the crisis of Fordism, it is hardly negligible, even if more intensive research in the area is needed. Thus, econometric work by Juillard (1988) reveals a downturn in productivity trends around 1967. Compared to the preceding period, which showed regular increases, the years that followed show a marked deterioration, which almost wipes out productivity gains at the level of the economy as a whole. Likewise, at the start of the 1970s, real wages also begin to decline, so that the distribution of productivity gains is impaired, not just their achievement. The plausibility of such a change is amply confirmed by more institutionally oriented analysis, which shows that both collective and "connective" bargaining break down (Coriat 1985). Increasing wage differentials, the decline of trade union power, and demands for wage givebacks despite the longest economic upswing since World War II all bear witness to this. To characterize the new system now emerging in a single phrase, American capitalism is in transition toward an extensive regime of accumulation with mass consumption (see table, p. xvi).

If we characterize each regime of accumulation as the combina-

TABLE 1. Four Regimes of Accumulation in Theory and History

CHARACTER OF ACCUMULATION	PREDOMINANTLY	
Character of consumption	*Extensive*	*Intensive*
Little integrated into capitalism	British economy 18th and early 19th centuries ①	American economy 19th century ②
Highly integrated into capitalism	American economy last third of 20th century ④	OECD economies post 1945 ③

tion of modes of production organization and of labor reproduction, then since the 1960s the United States has been entering a model of accumulation with no historical precedents. In this regime, the work force is increasingly dependent upon capitalism for its consumption, while the social and economic capacities of Fordist manufacturing organization and the expansion of services are constrained by difficulties in prolonging the logic of intensive accumulation, previously so effective. Viewed over more than two centuries, capitalism would thus be following a spiral path, successively expanding production and revolutionizing life-styles. Can, therefore, an accumulation process on an extensive basis, yet with mass consumption, prove to be a durable successor to Fordism? Nothing could be less certain, since Japan, South East Asia, and Europe all seem rather to be renewing the process of intensive accumulation with mass consumption, through the pursuit of increased productivity and a new transformation of industrial lifestyles.

As far as the American growth model is concerned, its dynamism has been based upon consumption, which has grown not only with the rise of credit, but with the increasing number of income sources per family. The rapid increase in the number of working women, especially in the tertiary sector, corresponds to the transformation of services previously available in the domestic sector into commodities. Similarly, highly paid jobs coexist with part-time work at wages well below those in industry (Bluestone and Harrison 1987). Once this is acknowledged, America's remarkable rate of job creation, so widely admired in Europe, appears largely due to the deepening of this dualism, or more precisely to the multiple tiering of the workplace, contrary to the Fordist principles of wage relations (Rosenberg 1988). All these are indices of a change in the regime of accumulation which marks a break with the previous "American way of life," the new one supposing a differentiation of life-styles based on sharp income inequalities (Steinberg 1986).

The mode of regulation was thereby destabilized, since most of the institutional forms, and the social patterns to which they gave rise, rested upon the dynamics of Fordism. An accommodating monetary policy, intended to lubricate economic growth, led to higher inflation and growing financial tensions in the United States and internationally. Under their combined effects, the international monetary regime has been in a state of breakdown since 1971, no new viable long-term configuration having emerged from the process of trial and error since then (Guttmann 1987). Along with monetary policy, the institutionalized compromises governing public spending and taxation formerly ensured that the government budget would balance over the typical business cycle. This was no longer the case once the process of intensive accumulation ran out of steam. Expenditures continued to increase, while the growth of the tax base slowed. This led to a deficit, requiring resort to money supply increases and/or foreign savings as households attempted to maintain their living standards by reducing their savings. The U.S. external deficit represents the logical consequence of these transformations. Manufacturing industry's structural loss of competitiveness, aggravated by a high exchange rate, was combined with the continued rapid expansion of domestic demand. From then on, there was a decided incompatibility between the conduct of American economic policy for internal ends and the viability of the prevailing international regime. The latter supposes some degree of stability in exchange rates, continuity in the rules of international commerce, and the possibility for the most endebted countries to meet their obligations.

Thus, although it may surprise the American reader, the members of the regulation school are inclined to hold to their earlier diagnoses. Though its crisis has endured since the late 1960s, the United States has not yet arrived at a viable regime of accumulation capable of preserving its hegemonic position in the international system. That unemployment reached its lowest level since the 1970s in mid-

1988 does not necessarily invalidate this diagnosis of structural crisis. It is certainly true that there have been many transformations of relations of competition, labor-management relations, monetary policy, budgetary priorities, and the tax system. However, it is not certain that the new combination of these structural forms constitutes a mode of development which can replace Fordism. Too many uncertainties still exist concerning the forms themselves, without even considering the macroeconomic disequilibria which must be resolved.

A Method, Not Just a Theory of Fordism

In fact, I hope that the present work will eliminate the principal ambiguity which has too often plagued the spread of the regulation approach. To many, it can be summed up as, if not reduced to, an analysis of Fordism. However, as the arguments above have implied already, Fordism is only one of the historical forms of the accumulation process, one which was preceded by others and which doubtless will be followed by another when the present crisis is overcome (if it is). Nor is the use of analysis in terms of regulation restricted to the older industrial capitalist economies. Applied to very different sorts of social formations, it has revealed a great variety of modes of development. Oil rent economies (Haussmann 1981), agricultural ones (Hillcoat 1976), small, open capitalist economies (Cassiers 1986), and the economies of dependent countries (Ominami 1980) display modes of development which have little to do with Fordism, whether peripheral, shackled, or incomplete.

In other words, the concept of Fordism is a product of the regulation approach, one which is provisional and subject to the limitations just noted. It is not the point of departure of the theory of regulation, much less the sum total of its results. On this point I can only refer the reader to chapter 2 of the present work. The final section of that chapter is an attempt to show that the regulation approach is a method of analysis, not a complete theory which represents an alternative to more ambitious constructs, whether neoclassical or Marxist in inspiration. This explains why the approach is open to a new generation of research. Without repeating the themes discussed in chapter 4, I will point out a few of the major questions facing it here.

If overcoming major crises depends on strategies and struggles concerning the organizational forms governing economic activity, and if one rejects any sort of strict economic or technological determinism, how can our understanding of these crucial episodes be advanced? Between the extremes of chance and necessity, there is a place for sociopolitical analysis specifying the determinants which transform institutional forms. This line of research can connect with the research in political science aimed at such objectives (Noël 1988; Drache and Glasbeek 1988). In passing, I should note a domain where such research has been particularly active and seemingly fruitful: that of urban sociology and economics. Begun by the work of Lipietz, it has attracted interest and advanced in the United States (Storper and Scott 1988).

New historical research could help clear up the puzzle represented by the great crises. Most works on regulation theory have been grounded on historical syntheses or monographs which made use of very different approaches. In addition, the availability of new economic time series and more detailed statistical analysis of previously available ones have cast some doubt on a number of claims, particularly those concerning the origins and stakes of the crisis of 1929 in the United States (Dumenil and Levy 1988). Along with this, might one not seek to formulate a gamut of macroeconomic models, incorporating both the real and financial determinants of accumulation, while correcting certain lacunae present in earlier formalizations? Such is undoubtedly one of the most important tasks to be undertaken, and it is to be hoped that specialists in American history on both sides of the Atlantic will play a part.

Toward New Theoretical Convergences?

The regulation approach is still clearly at a fairly early stage of its development, one which calls for constructive confrontations with other theories, both close to and distant from it. There is no point in repeating here the agenda for research sketched out in the final chapter of this book. I will limit myself to supplementing it with some specific references to research work in the United States which displays numerous convergences with that of the regulation school, even though it developed independently.

First of all, the new wave of research in radical economics in America has looked at many of the same questions examined by critical economists in Europe. Among explanations of the rise and crisis of the postwar economic regime, those of Bowles, Gordon, and Weiskopf (1983) and Reich, Gordon, and Edwards (1982) stress the specific characteristics of the labor-capital compromise, that between citizens and state around the welfare state, and the *pax americana* as the cornerstone of the international order. The parallels with the notions of the Fordist wage relation, institutional compromises and international growth regimes are evident. Their concept of "social structures of accumulation," for its part, appears to be the equivalent of those of regimes of accumulation or of modes of development. Another similarity lies in the fact that the intuitions drawn from the analyses of fundamental social relations led to the compilation of statistical evidence, some classical (real wages, productivity, profit rates), others novel (such as the American researchers' cost of job loss index).

The diagnosis of a structural crisis is also common to the two approaches, which distinguishes them from a number of traditional macroeconomic theories, for whom the upswing since 1983 marks the return of a strong, durable growth pattern. Their economic policy proposals also show some resemblances to ours, since both groups stress the imperative need for democratization, particularly in labor relations. However, some noteworthy differences remain, partly reflecting the differences in the institutional characteristics of the United States and Europe. Furthermore, hopes for growth through wage increases, the central proposition of *Beyond the Waste Land*, were cruelly disappointed by a number of social democratic experiments in Europe, France's 1981–82 reflation under Mitterand being illuminating in several respects. A number of encounters between the two approaches have already occurred, giving rise to common work (Bowles and Boyer 1988), and to parallel econometric studies (Weiskopf 1988; Peaucelle and Petit 1988).

With respect to institutional analysis of company organization and labor relations, another convergence can be noted. Long ago, the work of Piore and Doeringer (1972) detailed the macroeconomic consequences of a wage relation partially independent of the short-term pressures of the labor market. We owe the establishment of a connection between the American analytical tradition in labor relations and the regulation approach to Piore. Even more recently, together with Sable, he has analyzed both the history and future of economies of scale and of variety, and their consequences for industrial organization (Piore and Sable 1984). These authors' hypothesis of a swing to flexible specialization has stimulated a good deal of thought among members of the regulation school (Boyer and Coriat 1986). Nevertheless, the prognosis that Coriat and I arrived at continues to differ from that of our American colleagues. In our view, the introduction of greater product variety would represent a new phase of mass production, not its abandonment.

Another parallel can be drawn between the regulation approach and the systems of governance approach used by some American economists. Initially inspired by the theory of transaction costs, governance theory has undergone further development, producing some fruitful intersectoral and international comparisons. They underline the roles of the factors particular to each sector of the economy (the technology utilized, market structure, and the degree of internationalization) and of the socioeconomic determinants of choice, which are often particular to each social formation (Hollingsworth 1988). They also connect with one of the central questions in the social sciences, namely the relations between micro-level analyses and the findings of macroeconomic studies. The sector, representing an intermediate level, may be one of the keys to this transition, a fundamental issue at this stage in the development of regulation theory.

Of course, we should not forget the field of historical research. Some fairly remarkable convergences have appeared between our work and the preoccupations and methods of the theorists of corporatism. The same intent to connect economic performance with the characteristics of political organization and interest representation is present in the writings of both schools (Schmitter and Lembruch 1979; Berger 1981; Katzenstein 1984). An attempt to connect their work with the regulation approach would allow a better understanding of the origins of Fordism, and the subtle dialectics of its relationship with the corporatist regimes of the interwar period. It would also enable us to reach a better understanding of the strengths and limitations of the social democratic model and its numerous variants. In the light of the ideological transformations which socialist parties have undergone in the 1980s, these issues lead to an essential question. After the disappointments of liberalism, what forms of interest representation in the advanced capitalist economies can enable them to overcome the crisis of Fordism?

All these areas call for further research, which, it must be hoped, will occur on both sides of the Atlantic. I hope that such work will be encouraged by this publication of an English-language edition of my book, despite its imperfections (or perhaps because of them). Is it possible to analyze the development of the current crisis, and the conditions which might lead to its overcoming, now, without the comforting illusion of inevitability that historical distance allows? This is one of the major questions currently confronting the social sciences. In its own way, the theory of regulation may be one of the ingredients in the cauldron in which a renewal of critical social science is cooking.

Introduction to the French Edition

WHEN CRISES ENDURE, ORTHODOXIES FADE

If Rip van Winkle had slept through the past dozen years and awoke today, what changes in the economic and political landscape he would see! While inflation was previously the major preoccupation, concern today centers on the risk of deflation—an unheard-of phenomenon several years ago. If the principal debate in the 1970s was between Keynesianism and monetarism, in the 1980s liberalism reigns in every direction; one can only distinguish its conservative, centrist, and social democratic variants. A decade back, France's governments hesitated to restrain price and income increases, fearing that even a brief halt in the rise of living standards would prove socially unacceptable. Yet we have now experienced almost six years of stagnant incomes, as the 1982 "pause" in wage increases was transformed into a durable austerity policy. After the first oil crisis, decision makers' attention was focused on the risk of shortages, with steady increases extrapolated in the price of "black gold." Today, after the near breakup of OPEC, the world again seems awash in cheap energy, conservation programs are abandoned, and the construction of nuclear power plants is stopped or slowed.

In the mid-1970s, belief in the state's power to smooth out the business cycle was nearly universal. Conservative governments were no less willing than others to increase public spending and social insurance coverage, to finance a large share of infrastructural investment, and thus to offset decreases in private investment. Now, the time is long past when heads of government would say, with Richard Nixon, "We are all Keynesians now!" The prevailing slogans are rather: "Long live the market! Down with the state! Long live the flexible use of labor!" State intervention is regarded with suspicion; it is seen as intrinsically inefficient, a source of disorder and delays in the adjustments required by new technologies. Today, the economic policy of the entire world—even China!—could be summed up as: "liberalism, all of liberalism, and nothing but liberalism." In practice, this involves no more than the abolition of price controls, deregulation of the labor market, and disengagement of the state from economic activity (including some social insurance programs, and, in France, an historically unprecedented program of denationalization). But liberalism is no longer just an agreeable exposition of the virtues of a market economy. It has become the spearhead of an unprecedented program of *reforms*.

Difficulties which liberals still interpreted as "mere turbulence in a prosperous economy" in 1978 are now considered structural limitations to the various forms of intervention by the welfare state, which are held to inhibit necessary innovations by curbing the spirit of enterprise. The question is no longer one of fine tuning the system—by preferring a little more unemployment to a bit more inflation, or by giving priority to monetary policy over public spending. The stakes involve nothing less than constructing an economic and social system that will conform to the liberal ideal. However, a less superficial examination suggests that the problem is not quite so simple: for example, *no* school of economic thought has provided a satisfactory explanation for the surprising reversals in the economic situation between 1973 and 1985. Improvisation, tinkering, and groping seem to have been the rule. In fact, we have no equivalent to the Keynesian orthodoxy of the 1960s. Thus, in the United States, the most contradictory notions have succeeded each other since 1978. First came Milton Friedman—type monetarism, then Arthur Laffer's supply-side school, then Hayek-style fundamentalism. These were followed by movement toward a pragmatism that combined Keynesian reflation (through tax cuts and increased military spending) with rather restrictive monetary policy. A similar sort of oscillation was evident in U.S. international economic policy. After very severe constraints had been imposed on the debtor countries, the Baker plan, which reflected a recognition of the limits to adjustment through recession alone, sought a solution to the financial crisis in the most heavily indebted Third World countries through growth.

So we must bid farewell to all those lovely simple ideas and certitudes that made the economist, armed with a Keynesian model, statistical tools, and a national accounts time series into a demigod respected and followed by policymakers. In the mid-1980s, economists no longer enjoy such prestige: the term "distinguished economist" has once more taken on an ironic connotation. Yet appearances are deceiving in this regard. Where the nonspecialist sees only vain discourse about realities that escape analysis, the researcher is inclined to emphasize the *variety and richness* of the attempts that have been made to respond to the dual challenge posed by the crisis which has raised questions concerning both economic theory and economic policy. If the 1980s have been marked by the disappearance of the old orthodoxy, they are also characterized by some distinct innovations, as well as by the revival of neglected approaches.

TEN YEARS OF REGULATION THEORY

Times of crisis are times of *heterodoxy*, or, failing that, of the *synthesis of orthodoxies* in reaction to new problems. From this stems a paradox: an unprecedented resurgence of economic research has occurred even as it has become commonplace to speak of "the crisis of economic theory." In their own way, the approaches inspired by the concept of regulation make up part of this vast intellectual whirlpool. Melding a critique of orthodox Marxism with the Keynesian macroeconomic tradition, they have offered interpretations of our troubled era and some recommendations on how to overcome present dangers.

Neoclassical theory, today dominant within the discipline, is not the only possible approach for economic analysis. It is a theoretical system that regards crisis only indirectly, as a sort of absurdity. In the pure neoclassical model of the economy, all markets, including labor markets, tend toward equilibrium, thus ensuring full employment. If widespread, prolonged unemployment is observed, it can only be due to the violation of the model's underlying assumptions: complete rationality of individuals and firms, perfect information, and immediate coordination through simultaneous adjustments of price and quantity. Consequently, a crisis represents the difference between *theory* and *reality* in the economy in question, a result of the irrationality of consumers and workers (victims of monetary illusion, for example), inadequate information, or the blockage of market mechanisms by monopolies, labor unions, or interest groups that introduce rigidities leading to inflation and unemployment. From this comes a general conception of the economy in which any form of collective organization, state intervention, or regulation inevitably becomes a cause of crisis. It is apparent that standard economic theory treats institutions as would a learned Cosinus who applied his talents to social life:[1] if the facts don't fit the theory, scrap the facts!

Suppose, on the contrary, that the logic, origins, and disappearance of *institutional forms* were integral parts of a different way of approaching economics? This is precisely the starting point of theories of regulation. They make growth and crisis, along with their variability in time and space, the central questions of economic analysis, connecting these phenomena to the prevailing forms of social organization. Research on these questions, which began in the mid-1970s, sheds useful light on phenomena that orthodox theory considered obsolete: the recurrence of long-wave cycles and the marked slowdown in economic growth.

In short, structural crises have come back to plague us, and regulation theory was conceived in order to explain them. On that basis, a myriad of research projects developed. They gave rise to great expectations—in particular, to hopes for a rebirth of critical economics free from the grip of an increasingly fossilized Marxism. A decade later, perplexity, criticism, and even outright rejection of the approach have been the responses of many economists. A lack of novel results, an inability to develop satisfactory theoretical foundations, and weak economic policy proposals are said to explain why this approach has not given birth to a veritable school of thought, with its own rules of discussion, institutions, and dynamics. So what has become of it?

The present work is intended to provide an introduction to the regulation approach, and to put it into perspective. It is not meant to be just one more contribution to a rapidly growing descriptive literature. It is also intended as a critical discussion of the limitations and weaknesses of theories of capitalist regulation, and as an indication of the need for new research approaches. My contention is that regulation theory's current crisis of adolescence can be overcome if innovation prevails over the repetition of established ideas.

It is up to the reader to judge whether this ambition is legitimate, and to the interested researcher to contribute to the undertaking.

---

1. *Translator's note:* Cosinus is a French Ludwig von Drake: a comic strip academic who knows everything and understands nothing.

1. The Economic Crisis and the Resurgence of Theoretical Research

Two decades after the breakdown of the virtuous circle of growth of the 1960s, new prospects seem to have appeared. Although they remain uncertain, they point to far-reaching changes. Structural transformations of production and forms of economic organization, redefinitions of the ends and means of economic policy, and, above all, the multiplicity of analyses and theories that have more or less broken with Keynesian-neoclassical orthodoxy have shaped a set of debates—both intellectual and political. Thus, beyond the present crisis—the disappearance of the old order and the spread of doubts about previous images of reality—we must try to discern the seeds and outline of the emergent reconstruction of the economic and social terrain, and of economic theory itself.

I. THE TIME OF UNCERTAINTY

It has become conventional wisdom that the decline of oil prices and of the dollar presage a resumption of economic growth. However, this view confuses the causes of the immediate conjuncture (a short-run increase in economic activity) with the factors that determine long-term growth rates. It assumes that since 1973, the economies of the Organization for Economic Cooperation and Development (OECD) countries have suffered from a succession of ordinary recessions, which were merely deeper than usual and atypical because they resulted from the oil price increases. It means ignoring the obstacles that stalled the engines of growth: the slowdown in productivity increases and decline of profitability that began in the United States in the 1960s; the rising rates of inflation and the breakdown of the international monetary system; the increased competition among national economies (conflicts opposing Japan

1

and Europe to the United States as well as those between the newly industrialized countries and the old economies of the center); and last but not least, the foreign debt explosion.

Yet all of these structural disequilibria have hardly been eliminated. Industry and services have been substantially reorganized, but productivity trends have not improved significantly. Profits have picked up, but not investment, because the very success of anti-inflationary policies has pushed interest rates to levels that discourage the industrial investment required by the new technological order. The benefits of free trade have been repeatedly proclaimed, but we are witnessing the growth of creeping protectionism. Central banks have tried to guide the evolution of exchange rates, but the cooperation needed to establish a new international financial system remains lacking. Finally, the resolution of the debt problem is continually postponed, while recession—not faster growth—is used to bring international payments into balance.

It must therefore be recognized that the remarkable consistency between the dynamics of industry, finance, and the overall economy, the motive force behind the "thirty glorious years" that followed World War II, has today broken down. It is no longer a question of finding the "right" approach to short-term economic management, but one of seeking forms of economic organization and productive structures capable of promoting a durable resumption of growth and job creation. This explains, no doubt, the surprisingly rapid obsolescence that has overtaken most economic policies. The old opposition between Keynesian reflation through public spending and expansionary monetary policy nowadays seems quite outdated. At the beginning of the 1970s, governments' inability to combat unemployment and the rising inflation that derived from the various expansionary policies they pursued seemed to confirm the views of the monetarists. Wasn't inflation always a phenomenon primarily of monetary origin? But experience has shown that while control of the money supply—to the extent that it is possible—could certainly moderate or even stop inflation, the costs were considerable: the reduction of output, soaring unemployment, and declining industrial investment and residential construction. In other words, real economies—unlike the ideal ones of Milton Friedman–style monetarist theory—function far from the vicinity of full employment. Monetary policy has an effect on production and employment as well as on prices. Not to mention that financial innovations, which created a large variety of financial instruments as liquid as money but bearing interest, are capable of considerably distorting the relation between the total value of GNP and that of the means of payment, the touchstone of monetarist analysis. In this way, it became common in the 1980s to observe *both* rapid rates of increase in the money supply and low rates of inflation.

It therefore became important to analyze more precisely the determinants of output on the supply side as well as on that of demand. The supply-side school, for its part, emphasized the role of profitability in production and investment decisions, thus returning to one of the favorite themes of neoclassical thought. Back in the interwar crisis, this was the angle of attack chosen by Pigou, before Keynes offered an entirely different solution. But is it still possible to claim that supply always creates its own demand, ignoring what has been learned from several decades of monetary and macroeconomic theory? Moreover, we are still waiting for the empirical work that would prove that the advanced economies have crossed the threshold beyond which tax increases become counterproductive. Finally, numerous omissions and exaggerations in the economic policies recommended by this school have become evident. American experience in the 1980s clearly shows that a reduction in tax *rates* hardly stimulates an increase in total *revenue,* contrary to the marvelous formula that economists like Arthur Laffer proposed. As a result, this approach is far from constituting a new orthodoxy in economic policy.

In the end, a wide-ranging pragmatism has come to prevail in the 1980s. In fact, if official rhetoric borrows a great deal from conservative ideology ("Down with the state! Long live laissez-faire!"), governmental practice suggests a much more nuanced approach. To continue with the example of the United States, the slogans of deregulation and disengagement of the state from the economy have gone together in practice with interventions that, though selective, were nonetheless sizable. They included the unprecedented rescue of the Continental Illinois Bank, various sorts of interventions in labor relations (from breaking the air traffic controllers' strike to federal legislation codifying a minimum of workers' rights in response to the collapse of previous forms of collective bargaining), and an exceptionally high peacetime defense budget. The optimism that the American economy provoked after 1983, in contrast to a "sick" Europe, owed a great deal to the short-term recovery launched by the mixed marriage of classical Keynesian reflation (through tax cuts and public spending) and tight control over the money supply.

If the United States was able to pursue a policy that France was quickly forced to abandon in 1982–1983, it was because the country's trade deficit ceased to be a stumbling block once the attractiveness of the dollar—still the pivot of the international monetary system—drew massive capital inflows. Thus, rather ironically, Reaganism seeks to combine short-term Keynesianism with a long-term vision stressing initiative, competition, and profit as the driving forces of a new period of growth. At present, however, the outlines of this proposed new model remain utterly vague.

In other words, a "glorious uncertainty" about economic policy today prevails. But this situation is itself the indicator of a definite sense of malaise, frequently referred to as the crisis of economic theory. However, in this domain too, the waning of the old should not hide the scope of the efforts underway to find new approaches.

II. THE SEARCH FOR A NEW KEYNES

Indeed, the breakdown of the previous economic patterns, the structural transformations that resulted, and the mishaps that have befallen economic policies have attracted the attention of economic theoreticians. They have troubled both generalists and the specialists in various fields (such as monetary institutions, industrial economics, labor markets, and the theory of the firm). Consequently, numerous attempts have been made to resolve the contradictions between the predictions of different theories and models and the economic realities of the 1980s. This challenge faces the adherents of every paradigm, and sometimes divides currents of thought that until now were homogeneous. The keepers of existing orthodoxies are having trouble containing the criticisms and reformulations elaborated by sharpshooters on the margins of the established disciplines who seek to amend the old theories, elaborate new models, and even construct original paradigms.

It should not be surprising that the result is confusing. In effect, neoclassicists, neo-Keynesians, and neo-Marxists all confront the puzzle of the crisis on the basis of their own initial hypotheses and methodologies. At the risk of oversimplifying, one might describe the battle as pitting those holding to theories of rational behavior and self-equilibrating market adjustments against those for whom, by contrast, the very logic of contemporary economic systems is the explanation of unemployment and/or structural instability.

1. Rational Expectations:
Dr. Pangloss Meets Jean-Baptiste Say

Over the history of economic thought the hypothesis of individual rationality became increasingly central, to the point where it has come to constitute the cornerstone of modern theoretical constructs. However, the Keynesian model of effective demand and involuntary unemployment seemed to rest on ad hoc hypotheses—money illusion, the institutionalized rigidity of nominal wages, or myopic expectations. In response, many theoreticians have tried to find microeconomic (implicitly, "rational") bases for macroeconomic conditions involving unemployment. Thanks to Lucas (1984) and Sargent (1979) rational expectations theory has extended the hypothesis of individual optimization to anticipated reactions. In a universe characterized by stable relationships, economic agents will ultimately know the "true model of the economy," so that their errors of prediction can be due only to "surprises" and concern only the short run. The power of the critique of typical econometric models that this approach offers is evident. Because such models do not consider expectations—or learning behavior—they exaggerate the effectiveness of expansionary policies, since they consider effects that are only transitory (inflation, for example) to be permanent and indefinitely reproducible. But the positive contributions made by this school have been much more modest.

On the one hand, it is noteworthy that its claims regarding the transitory nature of the effects of economic policies depend not only on a most extreme view of the rationality of expectations (using available information as well as one can does not mean knowing "the true model" of whole economy!), but also on another hypothesis as formidable as it is debatable. In the medium term, prices and quantities on the various markets are held to adjust themselves so that all resources are fully utilized. However, Keynesian macroeconomic theory was founded precisely on the rejection of this postulate. Optimization by firms and employers and market adjustments may prove incapable of restoring full employment, once it is accepted that "supply does not create its own demand." In other words, the rational expectations school denies that prolonged unemployment can exist, and more generally denies the very possibility of the fallacy of composition, the foundation of macroeconomics, since it considers that any transaction that is advantageous at the microeconomic level must be so for the economy as a whole. Consequently, full employment can be attained through the cumulation of individual strategies, with no need for any coordination procedures besides the market. However, the paradox of the General Theory should be recalled: individual efforts to save prove are unable to increase investment and, on the contrary, reduce the level of employment.

On the other hand, this theory at best can explain the alternation of under- and overemployment, not long-term and growing unemployment ... unless a series of exogenous changes is invoked. At this point, Phelps' concept of natural unemployment is called in to fill the gap. Due to the constant movement of workers into and out of the labor market to seek better jobs, a permanent reserve of unemployed workers exists. Frictional in character, its size depends on the rate of departure from jobs and the time needed to obtain a new one. On this basis, the growth of unemployment is interpreted essentially as the result of workers' errors of perception regarding their real employment opportunities (a consequence of inflation, unemployment insurance, etc.). In practice, this means regarding unemployment that is essentially *involuntary* (layoffs, net reductions in jobs, etc.) as *voluntary*. Moreover, it interprets unemployment that has become *structural* as the simple quantitative expansion of a *transitory* status. The same criticisms apply to interpretations of the Phillips curve in terms of expectations. They lead to the recognition that the unemployment rate at which inflation stabilized did not stop rising until the end of the 1970s; but no explanation is provided for this development.

In sum, the new classical school does not offer a fully satisfactory explanation for the increasing rate and durable character of unemployment.

2. Investigations of the Labor Market: Whatever Happened to Structural Unemployment?

Precisely in order to explain the genuine puzzle that long-term unemployment represents for the central claims of neoclassical theory, in the past decade some studies have focused on the distinction between the wage relation and pure commodity relations. Thus, Azariadis' theory of implicit contracts introduces two major ideas to explain the inflexibility of nominal wages, even during recessions. First, wage earners may be more risk-averse than entrepreneurs. The maintenance of the existing wage level would then correspond to insurance against misfortune, obtained in return for lower pay when times are good. Second, the accumulated knowledge of the work force increases the entrepreneur's interest in retaining it, despite an unfavorable conjuncture that appears temporary. In both cases, labor is accorded a status different from that of a simple offer of services: the fact that workers remain with one enterprise for a long period gives rise to an enduring, internal logic of wage determination, opposed to the purely external and instantaneous logic of the market. Once this is assumed, wages no longer function to establish an equilibrium between labor supply and demand, but rather respond to firms' internal management objectives and workers' characteristics (their specific skills) and expectations (aversion to risk).

In sum, therefore, this original and sophisticated theory leads to a perfectly classical interpretation of unemployment. The agreed-upon wage determined in this manner would be higher than that which would ensure equilibrium on the labor market. Moreover, it can only explain temporary unemployment, the consequence of unexpected events that push down the "equilibrium wage," not long-term unemployment like that observed in both the 1930s and the 1980s.

Analyses in terms of efficient wages, like those of Stiglitz, also aim to show that the nominal wage is not the key adjustment variable on the labor market, but the argument explores another aspect of the wage relation. In this case, the emphasis is on the role of the wage in encouraging productive, efficient work. The separation of hiring on the labor market from the effective utilization of labor power in production is the essential point here. The payment of higher wages reduces absenteeism and turnover, while favoring the internalization by the work force of the firm's objectives regarding efficiency and returns (quality, productivity, timing, etc.). Thus, the wage level that renders the strategies of firms and workers compatible is generally higher than that which would permit full employment, while the existence of unemployment will not bring wages down to the latter level. This offers an explanation of the absence of automatic mechanisms ensuring the equilibrium of the labor market. The difficulty of obtaining full employment would thus stem fundamentally from the consequences of the distinction between purchasing labor power and putting it to use. Yet as interesting and stimulating as this theory may be, it leaves open the central question that concerns us here. It does indeed explain the existence of underemployment. But why did unemployment increase considerably, beginning in the 1970s? In this case, as in the preceding ones, note the

distance between a theory that is universal and timeless in scope
and an interpretation of an historical phase in which rapid growth
was followed by quasi-stagnation.

3. Disequilibrium Theory: The Difficulty of Establishing a New Orthodoxy

In a sense, these recent theories turn out to complement some older
ones that explain the possibility of unemployment through the absence of an auctioneer who would *simultaneously* adjust the set of
offers of supply and demand expressed on interdependent markets,
extending the logic of the stock market to the whole economy. This
is the point of departure for J.-P. Benassy–type disequilibrium theories (1984). They suppose that prices are initially fixed by reference
to a set of conventions or through planning procedures internal to
the firm, or at least that they tend to change less than the quantities
exchanged. Subsequently, economic agents seek to realize mutually
advantageous exchanges on the basis of this price system. In general,
supply and demand are not in spontaneous equilibrium. The surpluses and shortages observed thus feed back into the strategies of
the agents. A worker who has not found work shifts his consumption downward. A firm that could not sell its entire production will
reduce employment. From this results the possibility of an equilibrium of underemployment, in which unemployment and excess production capacity turn out to be compatible with rational, self-inter-
ested behavior by workers and firms. Optimization at the level of
the individual does not guarantee the attainment of full employment. It is nevertheless possible to speak of "disequilibrium" with
reference to the Walrasian concept of equilibrium, which would
ensure full employment through an appropriate price system.

This analytical framework thus connects two bodies of theoretical work: the neoclassical (through the utilization of the tools of
general equilibrium analysis) and the Keynesian (through its recognition of the *possibility* of persistent unemployment). But it is broader
than a mere reinterpretation of Keynes, since it can contain various
other configurations of the economy. In fact, unemployment can be
classical if the real wage is higher than productivity, and even *Marxian* if demand exceeds productive capacity, which is itself determined by past rates of profit. Finally, the price system and "autonomous" demand may be such that shortages of goods and of labor

prevail at the same time. Since resources are fully utilized in this situation, it can be termed one of *inflation*.

In this way, disequilibrium theory is even able to distinguish different types of crises and interpret the reasons for a swing from near full employment to persistent unemployment. Thus, a slowdown in productivity growth (at least in the United States) and a deterioration of the terms of exchange that *ought* to have produced a decline in wages were observed at the beginning of the 1970s. As such a decline did not occur, the Western economies suffered from unemployment—first classical, then Marxian—as the decline of profitability made its effects felt on investment. Malinvaud's proposed solution (1978, 1983, 1986) would therefore be to combine an incomes policy (or some other measure) that helps restore the place of profit in the distribution of income with support for demand through public spending.

Another interesting aspect of this approach is the possibility that crises may have various causes according to the historical phase in which they occur. In contrast with the classical (Marxian) unemployment of today, that of the 1930s would have been principally Keynesian in nature: excess productivity in relation to real wages, but insufficient demand, due, for example, to overly restrictive monetary or budgetary policies. Thus, disequilibrium theory has quite a few strong points in the race for recognition as a new orthodoxy: a rigorous reconciliation of micro- and macroeconomics, a synthesis of explanations previously considered incompatible, and original policy proposals which moreover, are, differentiated according to the structural conditions that produced the observed disequilibria.

Yet this approach is far from having gained general acceptance, at least internationally. When it has been discussed, it has most often been in an ultrasimplified form that emphasizes the classical character of present-day unemployment, not the alternation of Keynesian and classical unemployment (as most of the econometric work on disequilibrium suggests). No doubt the hypothesis of fixed prices, the basis of the theory, is repugnant to orthodox economists and has thus been interpreted as a weakness and peculiarity of this attempt to reconstruct macroeconomics. The theory of disequilibrium has encouraged the formulation of an oligopolistic theory of prices and wages, the development of institutionally oriented analyses, and attention to the dynamics of the wage-profit division and capital formation. However, outside of France, few economists have recognized the potential of this approach.

9

4. The Post-Keynesians: Financial Logic as the Source of Instability and Crisis

This short survey would be incomplete without a brief reference to post-Keynesian analyses in the manner of Minsky (1975, 1982), in which the origin of changes in the economy is essentially financial instability. In this view, modern economies are dominated by the choice between productive and financial investments, which is made on the basis of the present value of returns at the interest rate and the expected rate of profit. Thus, the best short-term strategy consists of taking advantage of low interest rates to build up debt and invest. But as the euphoria of boom spreads, firms accept ever-riskier financial schemes. At this point the slightest shock, apparently accidental, can reveal the latent disequilibrium between financial returns and the returns on productive capital, precipitating a crisis. The crisis may be cyclical: in other words, it may run its course after an acute phase, involving a race for liquidity among firms, followed by asset restructuring and, in some cases, bankruptcy. But it can also take on a cumulative form when the contraction of credit reduces overall demand rather than correcting the preceding financial speculation.

The crisis of 1929 offers a good example, not only of the absence of mechanisms ensuring equilibrium on the stock and financial markets, but also of the inverse process: the spiraling of crisis from credit to investment and production. Finally, in a third possible configuration, the tendency of debt economies to use inflation to postpone the appearance of the disequilibria between the real and financial spheres would lead to the complete inversion of the relationship between industrial and financial capital. The tightening of the monetary constraint would have the effect of raising the nominal rate of interest, halting the inflationary dynamic, and thus raising the real interest rate. In these conditions, physical investment would be halted, because financial investment or the consolidation of balance sheets would appear preferable, without even considering the direct effects of interest rates on firms' decisions regarding the formation of productive capital. The reader will have recognized here one of the characteristics of the 1980s.

Of course, this presentation offers a highly simplified, homogenized synthesis of theories that are quite varied, unequally formalized, and in some cases founded upon different traditions. But all are faithful to one of Keynes' key intuitions: that the full development of financial systems makes it even less likely that market economies will automatically arrive at equilibrium. Thus, economic instability and unemployment would not be the consequences of insufficient rationality among economic actors, contrary to the neoclassical tradition rehabilitated by the rational expectations school. Quite the opposite: they would be the expression of the logic of profit, rationally pursued through the increased sophistication and extension of financial instruments. Therefore, only through external intervention—by national central banks in the 1930s, and a supranational bank today—could expectations be stabilized and channeled or, more fundamentally, the conditions for steady growth reestablished.

Even this brief enumeration of some of the lines of inquiry pursued in response to the challenge presented by the distinctive features of the current crisis suggests the enormous variety of efforts economists have made. As one can see, if some have spoken of the "crisis" of economic theory, the period has been marked as much by the questioning of previous theories as by the emergence of new approaches—and the rediscovery of old ones.

III. FROM THE CRITIQUE OF ORTHODOXY TO THE RENOVATION OF MARXISM

In their own way, the approaches in terms of regulation make up part of this panorama. What is special about them is their theoretical inspiration, which begins essentially in the Marxist tradition, yet makes use of Keynesianism and economic history in hopes of renewing the institutionalist perspective and arriving at an original synthesis. Four major traits characterize the perspective.

1. Marx Is Dead. . . . But Not Buried!

The first of these is a certain fidelity to the methods and concerns of Marxist analysis. In an era in which the centennial of Marx's death has been the occasion for a critical reevaluation and general rejection of many of the previous readings of his work, it is worth recalling that Marx's legacy *still* constitutes a fruitful point of departure for social science research. The accent it places on *social relations* as the starting point for social analysis continues to represent one of the few alternatives to methodological individualism. When the question is the coherence (or the breakdown) of a society and its economic dynamics as a whole, the holistic method is far from useless. Besides, has it not furnished important results in anthropology, ethnology, and history—particularly economic history? The theorists of the regulation school start from the impact of a set of social relations (commodity and/or wage) on the stability of the economy. However, it is difficult to conceive of a pure theory of the economy—even a Marxist one!

2. Watch Out for the Laws About Tendencies!

Orthodox Marxism too often has succumbed to the temptation to believe that Marx had established the laws governing the long-term dynamics of capitalism once and for all. Thus, his successors have sought to demonstrate the existence of the tendency toward the deepening of capitalist crises, in particular due to the deepening of the capital-labor relationship and the declining rate of profit that it implied. Of course, dialectical analysis immediately reintroduced the factors that counteract the full effects of this law. But the danger then lay in juxtaposing a *theory* considered complete and finished— unfalsifiable in Popper's sense—to a sort of empirical *eclecticism*, which permitted the interpretation of *any* historical phase or conjuncture in terms of the theory.

This criticism is particularly relevant to the numerous variants of the concept of state monopoly capitalism, even though they represent an attempt to periodize the history of capitalism on the basis of forms of competition. But the same is also the case for research inspired by structuralism. If its critical merits regarding the fossilization and ideological usage of Marxism were welcome in the 1960s, its determination to reject all forms of historicism leaves it essentially ill-suited to the study of change or crises. In stressing the structurally invariant features of the capitalist mode of production, one neglects to analyze the changes that mark it. One underestimates its contradictions, to the point where history appears almost immobile. In reality, it is a spiral, a process of innovation and of reproduction according to modalities that change from one period to the next.

3. From Social Relations to Institutional Forms

Approaches in terms of regulation pay close attention to the precise forms that fundamental social relations take in a given society during a particular historical phase. Consequently, the central concept is that of institutional or structural forms. But, contrary to what these terms might suggest, they do not fall into the electicism of the school that bears the same name. Their Marxist origins lead them to emphasize a *structural* and *holistic* definition of these institutional forms. Fundamentally, all such forms derive either from the commodity relation, the labor-capital relation, or the interaction of the two. The lesser or greater extent of these two basic types of relations, along with their degree of maturity, are in fact capable of engendering different social configurations. A second hypothesis concerns the impact of these arrangements on the dynamism of the economy. Far from representing simple variants on an immutable set of mechanisms, they give rise to regularities in the accumulation process and in individual and collective behavior. One is thus led to seek to define different modes of regulation, in opposition above all to the notion of general equilibrium, but also to Marxist and structuralist conceptions of reproduction.

Under these conditions, the *present* crisis cannot be reduced either to the persistence of an equilibrium of underemployment (the usual Keynesian definition) or to the expectation of an imminent collapse of the whole of the system (the catastrophic version of the Marxist vision). Nor can it be reduced to a somewhat atypical business cycle (with Mitchell/NBER–type methodology), a viewpoint still current among American short-term analysts. The crisis is fundamentally the result of the economy's reaching the limits of the previous mode of regulation and the rise of contradictions within it. From this flows a specific task for the economist: to offer a precise characterization of the reasons why different phases succeed each other—phases of expansion and moderate cyclical fluctuations, followed by phases of stagnation and instability. In this view, the last two decades have been marked by the crisis of the "monopolistic" or "administered" mode of regulation which permitted the resolution of the crisis of 1929. In consequence—and this is one of the novel aspects of regulation theory—the economic policy problem of overcoming the crisis cannot be discussed in the abstract, that is, independently of the prevailing set of institutional forms. Furthermore, the issue is no longer mere tinkering with short-run policy, but rather promoting the emergence of an appropriate *mode of regulation*, a process in which the state may attempt to play a role, albeit less directly than indirectly.

4. Toward a Kaleckian Macroeconomics

But the regulation approaches do not stop at such general characterizations, because they also offer the elements of a *theory of macroeconomics*. Fundamentally, this theory is linked to the *accumulation of capital*. This is the fourth distinctive trait of the regulation approach. It is thus through a formal description of the profit-investment-capital-production-employment process (within two-section models of reproduction, for example, as well as within aggregated models) that it is possible to discover the nature of various regimes of accumulation and study their structural stability. In this way, regulation theory aims to give a renewed macroeconomics foundations that are more Kaleckian than Keynesian. First of all, its approach is more Marxist than neoclassical when it comes to describing the economic circuit. Second, the process of investment is conceived from a dynamic viewpoint, not from a static one as in the General Theory. Finally, its attention centers less on the stability of an equilibrium of underemployment than on the cyclical and/or cumulative movements of the economy.

Nevertheless, it shares three major ideas with the post-Keynesians. In the first place, the optimality of individual behavior does not ensure a convergence toward full employment. The stability of the whole does not equal that of its parts, particularly in a period of structural crisis. In the second place, macroeconomic analysis must take into account the specifics of the institutional arrangements of each period (for example, those concerning the capital-labor relationship) and seek policy instruments compatible with this configuration (such as the role of monetary policy when the nominal salary is downward-sticky). Finally, in particular historical moments, organizational forms that constitute obstacles to full employment must become the object of *structural reform*. In these cases, the objectives of economic policies will go beyond the short term, including medium- to long-term aims.

However, in their characterization of the current crisis, regulation theories offer a diagnosis that differs from both Keynesian orthodoxy and the analyses of Kalecki himself. These are connected to the fact that in a phase of intensive accumulation based on mass consumption, the economic system tends to confront limitations imposed by declining profitability, not insufficient overall demand. However, the latter is what the Keynesian theorists still maintain, tending to equate the present crisis with that of 1929 and to propose the same remedies. Nevertheless, the crisis is not simply a case of classical unemployment, as the disequilibrium theorists suggest. In fact, the wage-profit division is quite endogenous, and constitutes an essential component of the postwar regime of accumulation. Hence, to refer to the excess of real wages over productivity as "rigidity" is to turn a key element of the current system of regulation and regime of accumulation into a *deus ex machina*. As to the supply-side school, it brings us back to Jean-Baptiste Say and his sophisms: just what the regulation school is able to invalidate through its stress on commodity relations and the need to close the cycle of accumulation.

Before entering into a more systematic and detailed presentation of regulation theory in the next chapter, it may be useful to give a brief description of the school's development over the past decade.

IV. THE THEORY OF REGULATION: A BRIEF HISTORY

It is always difficult to draw up a balance sheet or sketch out a chronology for an intellectual tendency, particularly for someone who has been directly involved in it. The view point adopted must be thoroughly subjective, a function of personal choice. Nevertheless, it seems to me that five stages should be distinguished in order to understand the development of the strengths—and weaknesses—of the regulation approach.

1. Ambiguous Origins

We owe the introduction of the term "regulation" to Destanne de Bernis, who was one of the very first social scientists to use it. His work essentially aimed to use certain elements of systems theory to bring Marxist economic analysis up to date. It began with the definition set out by the philosopher Canguilhem, to whom regulation is "the adjustment, in conformity with certain rules or norms, of several movements or acts, and their effects or products, which are initially distinct due to their diversity or succession" (1980:1). Destanne de Bernis and the Research Group on the Regulation of the Capitalist Economy (GRREC) devoted themselves to describing the different norms and adjustment variables specific to capitalism. They argued that the rule of the maximization of the rate of profit makes itself felt through two major tendencies—namely the declining rate of profit and the equalization of sectoral rates of profit. As to the variables, they were put in three categories according to their manner of development:

- *Regular:* those involving population, technological progress, the growth of the size of firms, and the extension of the space dominated by capitalism.

- *Subject to short-term fluctuation:* chiefly the variables of price and quantity, which change according to specific laws.

- *Subject to discontinuous evolution:* essentially institutions, defined by Hauriou as representing the results of a social armistice after a phase of conflicts and struggles (such as forms of competition, state intervention, etc.).

When these three sets of variables are articulated into a coherent whole, it is possible to speak of the *mode of regulation* associated with a given period of economic history. This presentation of the subject was provocative and useful. It inspired—positively or negatively—a large body of subsequent work.

However, the approach was not without ambiguities and weaknesses. First, it presents a series of tendencies that are far from evident as perfectly well established, thus giving a rather teleological character to the argument. Second, Destanne de Bernis' Grenoble research group reintroduced the falling rate of profit as a law, when in reality no mode of regulation is viable unless it counteracts this tendency. Finally, its suggested periodization of economic history, as well as its policy conclusions, were very close to those of the state monopoly capital school.

Doubtless it was due to these works that the theory of regulation came to be seen by some as nothing more than "old Marxist theory in new clothes." One of the factors that favored this perception was the preponderant role that it accorded to *the form of the state*, to the point where one could have the impression of a single decision-making center that is relatively conscious of the long-term interests and necessities of the system. Consequently, the divergence between the international sphere—the level at which accumulation occurs—and the conjunction of national spaces (nation-states) would explain the novel features of the present crisis compared to that of the 1930s. No one doubts that this factor is important, but what then is the significance of the regime of accumulation itself? The works of the Grenoble group sometimes give the impression that regimes of accumulation remain invariant over the long run; only the institutions supporting them change without affecting their nature. In the end, the notions borrowed from systems theory proved to offer no more than a metaphor and a heuristic principle, not a starting point for a precise, quantified analysis of the dynamics of accumulation.

2. A Pathbreaking Work

Indeed, subsequent work in this field was based upon a second theoretical pillar, the approach elaborated by Michel Aglietta, initially in his thesis, and later in *A Theory of Capitalist Regulation: The U.S. Experience* (1976). He distinguished his work sharply from the systems approach, whether cybernetic or thermodynamic, arguing forcefully that it is impossible to articulate "a metadiscourse on organization independently of content or roots in a specific reality" (1982:111). Likewise, he put considerably less emphasis on the concept that regulation was the consequence of increasingly diversified state intervention in the economy. If Aglietta shared Destanne de Bernis' desire to find an overall alternative to general equilibrium theory, he differed in his rejection of abstract economic laws. On the contrary: by pursuing the hypothesis that the object of social science is social relations, he arrived at the notion of the *structural form* as the codification of a set of fundamental social relations. From this point on, his research became extremely ambitious, since its objective amounted to "the study of the transformation of social relations, which creates new forms—both economic and non-economic —organized in structures and reproducing a determinate structure, the mode of reproduction" (1982:14).

Aglietta begins with theoretical reflections on the most fundamental Marxist categories, such as the value of labor power, which he sees as determined by the intersection of the reigning norms of consumption and the rate of exploitation resulting from the accumulation process. Likewise, the status of money, the role of credit, and the effects of inflation on accumulation receive special attention in his work. But its essential originality involves *the linkage of this theory with the economic and social history of the United States.* It is thus the study of the emergence and significance of collective bargaining that leads him to forge the notion of consumption norms and to see the dynamics of the economy as the result of their interaction with the norms of production. Likewise, he connects the transformations of large-scale firms with characteristics of the regime of accumulation and the dynamics of profits. Once this is done, the present crisis can be interpreted as a divergence between the norms of consumption and production. *Inflation* is the particular form that it takes, an apparent attempt to postpone these disequilibria. In this author's first work, the *commodification* of the collective elements involved in the reproduction of the work force was presented as one of the possible motive forces in the constitution of a new regime of accumulation.

3. Establishing an Agenda for Research

Even if it took six years before the first French edition of *A Theory of Capitalist Regulation* sold out, the book had a substantial impact on Aglietta's colleagues, receiving countless citations and favorable references. Among those influenced by it, the work of the Center for Mathematical Economic Forecasting Studies Applied to Planning (CEPREMAP) and the Production Systems Research Group (GRESP) must be mentioned, along with the contributions of Billaudot and Bertrand. They pursued and unified the line of research that began with Aglietta's study of the long-term dynamics of the United States economy, making contributions at four different levels. First of all, the same questions and methods inspired research on capitalism in France and in the major OECD countries. These studies were not mere repetitions, for they produced novel results that went beyond Aglietta's initial work. Thus, the notion of the regime of accumulation was examined more thoroughly and formalized, giving rise to a greater variety of configurations than those observed in the United States. Likewise, the specific characteristics of present-day intensive accumulation (that is, accumulation in which production and consumption norms evolve simultaneously) were analyzed by both Bertrand (1976) and Billaudot (1978). Secondly, the collective research by CEPREMAP members on inflation (1977) produced clearer distinctions between the notions of structural form, regime of accumulation, and mode of regulation. Historically, of course, competitive regulation has been associated with extensive accumulation, followed by monopoly regulation with intensive accumulation involving mass consumption. However, other combinations are theoretically possible, and in particular must be studied if one wishes to examine possibilities for resolving the present crisis. Moreover, the concept of regime of accumulation is situated at a fairly high level of abstraction (that of coercive laws imposed on the system as a whole), while the mode of regulation operates at a level evident to the general public, to follow the distinction established by Alain Lipietz.

But the contributions of these authors also lie in the areas of methodology and results. Detailed studies of the various forms of institutions and social reproduction—followed by description of the relations between them—required more elaborate tools for verifying and applying theory. As a result, quantitative work, guided by institutional studies, became more thorough, enabling researchers to test the validity of their intermediate hypotheses. For example, they learned that classical competitive regulation can coexist with prematurely monopolistic institutions. Such was the case in France in the interwar years, both with respect to wage determination and the dynamics of prices and profits. With this methodology, the viability of an historical mode of development can be rigorously studied without postulating a priori either its structural instability or its spontaneous equilibration. On that basis, conclusions and *periodizations* can be made more precise and pertinent. At the same time, detailed analyses spelled out the sectoral dynamics to which the evolution of the aggregates corresponded, the work done by GRESP being exemplary in this regard. With regard to the origins of the present crisis, the contributions of various factors ranging from declines in productivity to the growth of the tertiary sector and the state, as well as the exhaustion of the norms of consumption, can be evaluated and discussed, as Lorenzi, Pastré, and Toledano (1980) have shown.

Did this represent the beginning of a real *research program* in Thomas Kuhn's sense? That is for everyone to judge after reading this work—and those which came before it. But there are also more negative aspects that it would be foolish to conceal and that, moreover, have not escaped the attention of critics.

19

4. Bad Regulation Theory Drives Out the Good

If we now leave the small circle of direct contributors to this approach, what we can see is completely different. No doubt it was the fate of a term that was so attractive, yet general, to suffer an unfortunate sort of popularization. It is regrettable that the same term has in fact three meanings that are completely different, and indeed opposed:

- Regulation as a concept in *systems theory*, biology, and thermodynamics: a potential basis for a theory of organization, as understood at the Cerisy conference.[1] As I have suggested however, for the moment the relation between this use of the concept and its use by economists is only an analogy, and therefore somewhat superficial.

- Regulation as conscious and active intervention by the *state* or other collective organizations: on the macroeconomic level, this means a *Keynesian* policy of economic stabilization, and on the sectoral level, the growth of *governmental rule making*. But in that case, why not use these two terms, which are more precise and contain no ambiguity?

- Regulation as the conjunction of the mechanisms working together for social reproduction, with attention to the prevalent economic structures and social forms: the present work is concerned only with this notion. It is easy to see that it represents the core element common to the various currents of thought within the regulation school, despite the significant differences between them.

This diversity of meanings predictably led to a multiplicity of references to the term "regulation," giving rise to undeniable confusion. Two examples will show this. In the economic scenarios set out during the preparation of the late, lamented Eighth French Plan, a policy of laissez-faire was opposed to another called "regulation" simply in order to suggest much more active intervention in terms of public spending, credit policy, and taxation. Some ill-informed

1. *Translator's note:* The Cerisy conference on models of self-organization brought together researchers in various disciplines interested in models of systems and regulatory processes. Papers presented there were published in P. Dumouchel and J.-P. Dupuy, eds., *L'auto-organisation: De la physique au politique* (Paris: Seuil, 1983).

observers (for example, students—including advanced ones) interpreted this as a success for the regulation school! A second, equally significant anecdote: when one seeks to translate this notion into English, one comes up against the absence of adequate terms. Consequently, because they are homonyms, the idea of regulation is assimilated to that of administrative rule making, which also translates as "regulation." From this has arisen the impression that the whole approach is no more than a variant of Keynesianism or the institutions established under the New Deal! As to the confusion with systems theory, and indeed catastrophy theory, it has sometimes been encouraged by the regulationists themselves, so difficult is it to resist an image that seems apt, even at the price of a double entendre and a subsequent series of misunderstandings.

But that is certainly not the worst: this blurring, indeed almost total loss, of meaning is, after all, the price of success. It is on the other hand more disturbing that some young researchers have thought that the founders of the regulation school had already resolved any problems that might appear in their own fields of research. I will not comment further here on the exam bluebooks which, no matter what the question posed, chant the well-known refrain, "Long live regulation and its Holy Apostles!" Rather, I will cite two pieces of research that fell into this trap. In one, a study of the long-term growth of the female work force limited itself to establishing a purely mechanical correspondence between the succession of regimes of accumulation and the ways in which women were drawn into the labor force, without any original contribution sketching out the logical relations between the character of the mode of regulation and the status of working women. But there is an even graver— almost surreal—case of such misappropriation. A Mexican colleague who had been impressed by *Accumulation, inflation, crises* (Boyer and Mistral 1978) managed the tour de force of applying the book's conclusions concerning the nature of the contemporary crisis in France to Mexico, at the same time providing statistical tables that completely invalidated the thesis presented. The fidelity of the transposition thus led him to conclude that the rate of profit fell in Mexico after 1976 (as Mistral and I had said), ignoring what were in reality the first signs of a completely different crisis. Such an error is especially revealing in that one of the major lessons that the regulation theorists drew from the *Annales* school (particularly Labrousse) is precisely the maxim that "every society has the crises and conjunctures which correspond to its structure."[2]

Does Gresham's law also apply to economic theories and ideas? In any event, it must be recognized that such a use of theory is completely sterile and counterproductive; indeed, it inhibits genuine, properly conducted research. Must the exponents of the ideas of the regulation school be considered responsible? Those observers who consider it to be no more than the combination of limited analyses with poorly established results would say so, especially, since the most recent works give the impression of a great dispersion of views within the school.

5. Contemporary Research: Profusion or Incoherence?

Since the beginning of the 1980s, numerous works and articles by the principal figures using the regulation approach have appeared. But there are two possible readings of this, reflecting opposing interpretations of the development of the school.

It can be viewed as a sign of maturity and of the extension of a theory still being constituted to new fields of analysis. In this respect, the optimists can express a certain satisfaction. In labor economics, regulation approaches have joined the concept of segmentation to become the implicit point of reference for various pieces of fieldwork. In this connection, the remarkable convergences between this perspective and the work of a series of American authors who have studied the problems of dual labor markets (Piore 1979) and divisions in the work force (Reich, Gordon, and Edwards, 1982) should be underlined. Thus study of the transformations of the wage relation since 1973 has revealed the growing heterogeneity of the forms it takes, both between different categories of workers and different countries. While regulation theorists thought initially in terms of uniform institutional forms, today they speak of the articulation of a large variety of forms represented by a model type. Likewise, studies concerning Chile, Venezuela, Mexico, and other developing countries have clearly shown the *diversity of modes of regulation* and therefore of the exact forms that crises take. This

2. *Translator's note: Les Annales* is France's leading journal of economic and social history, established in the 1930s. The *Annales* school, including historians such as Ernest Labrousse and Fernand Braudel, is known for its attention to social groups, phenomena, structures, and data sources ignored by traditional elite-oriented history.

differentiation prevails among European countries as well, explaining a large part of their relative competitiveness and growth rates, even though they are subject to shared rules and a common environment. Finally, the accent has moved from simple analysis of the past to a more forward-looking examination of the issues involved in the current crisis and of problems of economic policy. It is significant, for example, that the most recent publications by Aglietta and Brender, Lipietz, Mazier, Baslé and Vidal, and my own recent work conclude with policy discussions and proposals that are considerably more detailed than in preceding ones. Prediction also constitutes a particularly demanding test, which in fact required the greater refinement of existing tools, such as those used for macroeconomic modeling. Topics such as the viability of more competitive arrangements for salary determination (Boyer 1986a) and flexibility in management (Boyer and Coriat 1986) can only be discussed on the basis of a study of the rate and stability of growth within a *formal macroeconomic model*.

But other writers have drawn quite different conclusions after reading the same works. They interpret the growing number of national case studies and the discovery of a degree of heterogeneity in institutional forms as a sign of the *weakness* of the theoretical model and the reduction of the explanatory schema to a mere description. Yet other observers, although their critique is not as far-reaching, argue that the regulation approach offers an underdetermined model of the economy which requires the introduction of other explanatory factors. More fundamentally, the question is posed of the *consistency* and *homogeneity* of the different works that claim to use the regulation approach. In this connection, the perplexity of a reader attached to simple ideas could be increased by two peculiar aspects of these works.

On the one hand, the underlying foundations of the analyses of a given author may vary quite considerably. Thus, Aglietta adhered to the Marxist theory of value in his 1976 book, but subsequently abandoned it in *La violence de la monnaie* (1982) and *Les metamorphoses de la société salariale* (1984). Furthermore, what he considered a structural crisis in 1976 he called a simple change in the mode of development in 1984. On the other hand, in the mid-1980s, economists using the regulation approach do not all rely upon the same theoretical foundations. For example, the theory of value is clearly Marxist in Lipietz, implicitly individualist through the usage of a Girardian approach in Aglietta, and unspecified for other authors, such as Boyer and Mistral. For anyone who conceives of the history of economic ideas as a struggle between objective and subjective theories of value, such ambiguity is utterly unacceptable. Lastly, while the economic policy recommendations of the school's members undoubtedly have a common nucleus, they also diverge on specific points. Thus, on trade policy, pleas for a well-tempered protectionism (Lipietz) are juxtaposed with analyses that consider some form of free trade to be the least bad system (Mistral's most recent position). More generally, the lack of precision in the regulation school's recommendations concerning exchange rates, tax policy, and public spending makes economists of other persuasions say that in the last analysis, its members have no program to resolve the crisis.

From the perspective of such skeptics, the regulation approach would constitute a *misguided version* of the institutionalist school. But, they say, the history of economic thought has repeatedly shown that school's inability to set out an alternative paradigm and sustain a cumulative flow of work. Worse still, regulation theory might simply be a fad deriving from the intellectual isolation of French academics, who are far from the mainstream of debate in social science at the international level.

The purpose of this book is to attempt to show that such is not the case. The regulation approach does not aim to describe the world as it is, but to theorize certain aspects of it. It has found parallel currents of thought or echoes in other countries, including America, among radical economists. Furthermore, its methodology can give rise to a second generation of studies, which, building on what has already been learned, can address the new questions raised by the depth and duration of the current crisis.

2. Regulation Theory: A User's Guide to Concepts and Methods

Readers who want to make up their minds about the regulation approach face at least three kinds of difficulties.

First, it is noteworthy that most of the stands economists have taken concerning the regulation school have been based on a very *incomplete* knowledge of the works it has produced. During most of the 1970s, the essential papers were available only in mimeographed form. The publication of articles and syntheses based on the regulation approach has become more frequent only in the past seven years. Even today, economists generally read and cite only the works that are closest to their main research interests (Marxist theory in general, labor economics, macroeconomic modeling, economic history, etc.) It may therefore be useful to offer a presentation and synthesis (and if possible, a dissection) of the principal concepts used by most members of the school and in most fields. Such is the first aim of this chapter.

Next, the observer who plunges into the works of the regulation school risks coming to a fairly simple diagnosis of the causes of the current crisis. Basically, all of its members have reached the same conclusion, repeated and amplified in a web of mutual citations: the break with previous economic trends after 1973 derived from the *crisis of Fordism* as an economic, social, and technical principle of organization. But the most critical readers will recognize that this result is neither very original nor particularly well argued in terms of empirical detail. From this has come the idea that the success of the regulation approach has been no more than a fashion, a wildly exaggerated beating of the drums in relation to its real contributions. However, this chapter seeks to show that such a view mistakes *one result*, admittedly an important one, for the *overall approach*. Thus, I will concentrate here on presenting a methodology that can be applied at points far apart in time and space. These may include

periods quite different from that marked by the Fordist mode of
development and monopolistic regulation, which have characterized
only the older industrialized capitalist countries during the past four
decades. My aim is that the tree should hide neither the seed (the
method) nor the forest (the various results produced).

Finally, well-informed readers and specialists who have followed
the evolution of the approach step by step may encounter yet another source of confusion. If the objective of the regulation school
until the early 1980s was the critical renovation of Marxist economic analysis, they may ask: haven't its theoretical frames of reference become widely dispersed since then? In fact, depending on
the author or the object of analysis, Girard, Keynes, Marx, and even
the founders of the institutionalist school may be invoked to provide
a basis for the concept of "structural forms" and to justify the notion
of "modes of regulation." However, since such diverse points of
reference appear contradictory, they may be viewed as indicating a
loss of the substance and dynamism of what might have constituted
a school.

This tension does indeed exist, but it must be kept in perspective.
The conflicts involve the most abstract economic concepts underlying the intermediate categories used by the members of the regulation school in their empirical work. But broad agreement exists
concerning the *core* of these intermediate notions.

It may well be, for example, that the theory of value used by some
members of the school does not make much difference concerning
the questions with which they deal. It may suffice to accept that,
under capitalism, the conjunction of the commodity relation and the
wage relation makes the equivalent of the price of production the
regulator of the dynamics of market prices, following the views of
Medio and Johansen. According to certain hypotheses, the objective,
subjective, and symmetrical theories of value lead to the same conclusions (cf. the theorems of nonsubstitutability). Hence, macroeconomic analysis can work from this result without directly concerning itself with theories of value. More generally, one can argue that
virtually all of the theorists of the regulation school agree on a set of
intermediate concepts that can be inserted into completely different
theoretical frameworks. The present chapter is an attempt to demonstrate the validity of this approach.

Nonetheless, it would be pointless to deny that such a synthesis
is quite personal. In particular, it corresponds to the approach that
underlies, at least implicitly, most of my previous work. However,

this chapter also means to find common ground among members of a school who display a great deal of variety. The argument will involve specifying the issues in the analysis, defining the basic concepts, showing their articulation, and finally spelling out a method for putting them to use.

I. THE CENTRAL QUESTION: THE VARIABILITY OF ECONOMIC AND SOCIAL DYNAMICS IN TIME AND SPACE

Attempts to construct theory depend, in a sense, on the question which the economist intends, explicitly or implicitly, to answer. Theories of regulation, for their part, have developed in response to three of the major quandaries confronted by the various schools of economic analysis described in the last chapter.

1. *Why and how does a given economic formation shift from strong, steady growth to near stagnation and an unstable series of short-run patterns?*

The paradox here stems from the fact that most economists accept the notion that markets are naturally self-regulating. If that is the case, crisis can only be an accident, due to an unpredictable conjunction of unfortunate occurrences or sociopolitical interference. But can one then understand the long-term dynamics of market economies without focusing on the changes in their relations with the whole of the sociopolitical system, which sometimes stabilize and sometimes destabilize their short-run behavior, as Polanyi emphasized? Yet it is not enough to declare, to the contrary, that the tendencies toward crisis and stagnation in mature capitalism are ineluctable. It then becomes necessary to explain why, for example, unprecedented growth was possible in the old industrialized countries after World War II. As we have seen, adherents of orthodox, neoclassical, Keynesian, and Marxist approaches have all had some difficulty in explaining such a qualitative change in the determinants of growth and the business cycle.

2. *How can we explain that within a particular historical era, crisis and growth take significantly different forms in different nations, to the extent that disequilibria can deepen in some countries while others are relatively prosperous?*

Undoubtedly due to the studies underlining the ties resulting from the internationalization of trade, production, finance, and currencies, the short-term behavior of each economy is often thought of as the projection (almost in the mathematical sense of the term) of a logic that is only apparent at the level of the international (or world) system. But one frequently moves from the assumption of interdependence to that of homogeneity, or, at least, of the strict hierarchization of the determinants of growth and crisis. When this happens, national specificities tend to disappear, and the contradictory unity of the factors of cohesion and division within the international economy is lost from sight. However, the history of the past three decades underlines the breadth of the differences among countries. Haven't growth rates been unequal among the dominant OECD countries since the mid-1950s? Since 1973, haven't we witnessed opposing tendencies at work in the old industrial countries and the newly industrialized countries? Finally, since 1982, haven't the differences in the evolution of the economies of the United States, Japan, and Europe been patently manifest in the differences in their growth and unemployment rates? Once this is acknowledged, economists need much finer approaches that allow them to examine these differences and indeed to explain them with their theories and models.

3. *Finally why, beyond certain general regularities, have crises taken different forms over time, for example, in the nineteenth century, in the interwar period, and in the present day?*

In fact, this is really two questions. Given the place that the notion of crisis occupies in most economic theories—often minor, and sometimes nonexistent—is there not a tendency to assimilate depression to a simple phase of a fluctuating, almost cyclical process whose function is to purge the economy of disequilibria that preceded it? But then how is it possible to explain durable changes in growth rates, let alone the sort of enduring stagnation and erratic short-term fluctuations of which the 1930s offer a striking example? In short, the term "crisis" may refer to quite distinct theoretical objects, depending on whether one is interested in Juglar cycles, Kondratiev long waves, or Kuznets' quasi-secular movements. On the other hand, if one does distinguish the short-run conjuncture from the medium or long term, there is a strong temptation to consider the archetype of the great crisis to be the dramatic crash of 1929, which was exceptional in its depth and duration. However, a point-by-point comparison of that crisis with the present situation would suggest that despite certain similarities (overproduction, the decline of profitability, record interest rates and unemployment levels), there are notable differences. In the current crisis, inflation initially continued, then was stabilized (as opposed to the rapid, brutal deflation that followed 1929), and short-run economic and trade trends have differed (the absence of cumulative depression and the contraction of exports, along with continuing import penetration of domestic markets). These changes represent more than mere epiphenomena, and they call for a theory that allows us to explain them.

In fact, these three paradoxes all fall within one general question: *how economic and social dynamics vary over space and time.* From this stems a problem of method at the meeting point of two traditionally distinct disciplines: economic history and economic theory.

II. TOWARD A FRUITFUL DIALOGUE BETWEEN ECONOMIC HISTORY AND THEORY

Part of the difficulty in responding to the three problems described above lies in the division of intellectual labor between these two disciplines—which, though longstanding, is nevertheless harmful. For the historian, the essential task is the elaboration of historical facts. Other disciplines—economic analysis, in particular—offer tools rather than an overall approach. For the economist, on the contrary, history and international comparisons furnish data for testing the theoretical models drawn from logical analysis or postulates. But it is rare that stubborn empirical evidence will lead to the rejection of a system of interpretation, or even to its modification.

In a sense, historical research sometimes gives the impression of not having completely overcome the inadequacies of an event-oriented approach, which used to center on political history. Certainly, since the rise of the *Annales* school, its objective has been the analysis of the relations among economic, political, religious, and psychological structures. The critical analysis of documents is thus no longer the only aspect of the historian's work, since it must be related to a carefully defined question and the testing of one or several hypotheses. Economic historians therefore always take care to restrict the validity of their results, which they often limit to one epoch, a single place, and a particular phenomenon. It is quite rare that they allow themselves to use theories from other disciplines to resolve difficulties encountered while working on their monographs. Most of the time, these difficulties are attributed either to the imperfections of the sources or to the particular characteristics of real socioeconomic structures and events compared to the abstractions of "pure" theory.

Economists, for their part, rarely display such modesty. Trusting in the venerable character of the concepts they utilize, and in the logical rigor that enables them to deduce individual behavior or laws from a few first principles, they are tempted to regard any divergence between historical developments and the teachings of their theories as inconsequential, no matter how gaping it may be. Is it not precisely the role of theories and models to go beyond historical contingency to establish continuities and recurrent patterns? Thus, unlike their historian colleagues, economic theoreticians are not very inclined to change their systems of interpretation in response to conflicting data. On the contrary, such conflict represents an incitement to persevere, even at the price of defining new measurements or methods that allow historical reality to fit the theory. The testing of the quantity theory of money against the monetary history of the United States or the United Kingdom illustrates the permanent temptation to validate the central hypothesis of the theory through marginal amendments or ad hoc additions to the initial model. Such is the role that the variability of the velocity of circulation of money seems to play. The same would hold for the succession of definitions of what the "true" money supply actually is.

Of course, the opposition between economists' and historians' approaches is not as absolute as the preceding remarks would suggest. On the one hand, some economic theorists have always tried to use long-term historical data to understand the origins of certain national peculiarities and of crises, seeking to establish a regular interplay between the elaboration of concepts and their confrontation with historical reality. For their part, some unorthodox Marxists have long looked for ways to establish a fruitful dialectic between Marx's concepts and intuitions and economic transformations since the time of *Capital.* It is noteworthy that they have elaborated new concepts that lie in an intermediate range between pure abstraction and empirical verification. On the other hand, the *Annales* school was constituted in reaction to a certain dogmatism on the part of official Marxism, during a troubled time that encouraged a new look at historical eras analogous in their economic fluctuations and social transformations. Since then some historians have tried to construct a coherent overall system of interpretation based on a multiplicity of local studies but global in intent. Thus, Fernand Braudel, for example, presented new ideas on the theory and stages of capitalism (such as the precedence of merchant capitalism over industrial capitalism) which were sometimes opposed to the prevailing orthodoxies. But today such vast syntheses have become rare, and not only because they require extraordinary individuals. In our day, most researchers restrict themselves to an event-oriented history which, while extending its investigations to new spheres of social life, rarely poses the problem of the totality of the socioeconomic system.

Using long-term historical data to enrich and critically elaborate Marxist intuitions concerning the dynamics of capitalist economies is the aim of the regulation approach. If it is always stimulating to start from Marx's teachings, a decade of research has permitted the establishment of hierarchies within his legacy. We can distinguish between the most abstract concept (mode of production, wage labor, etc.) and those that can and must be tested against observed phenomena (for instance, the stability or instability of a partial mode of regulation, the cyclical or structural character of a crisis, etc.); between a social relation in general and the specific forms that it takes over time; and between laws that hold true across history and simple economic regularities valid for a specific set of social forms.

III. ESTABLISHING A HIERARCHY OF INTERMEDIATE CONCEPTS

In fact, the difficulties discussed above stem largely from the unjustifiable domination that the two extremes of abstraction and empiricism have enjoyed in economic discussions. The problem is therefore to construct different sorts of concepts, which allow us to move from the highest level of abstraction to propositions that can be tested against research material or social actors' immediate life experiences. This has been precisely the aim of the research work which, despite considerable diversity in approach, is grouped together under the rubric of "the regulation approach." At the risk of greatly simplifying a history that is actually far richer, it is illuminating to distinguish three levels of analysis and place them in hierarchical order, thus establishing a classification of the various concepts that make up the theories of regulation.

31

1. The Starting Point: Modes of Production and Their Articulation

It is useful to begin with Marx's celebrated statement: "In the social production of their life, men enter into definite relations that are indispensable and independent of their will, relations of production" (Preface to *A Contribution to the Critique of Political Economy*). Nevertheless, I will not accept the two affirmations that complete this passage. First, it is certainly abusive to establish a strict correspondence between the relations of production and a given level of productive forces. Second, the dichotomy established between the economic structure and the juridical and political superstructure tends to prevent social analysis from getting beyond the notion of determination "in the last instance" by the economy and the state of the productive forces.

Emphasizing the relations of production has the advantage of avoiding any possible confusion between the rivalries among individuals seeking to occupy positions within a mode of production and the general social frameworks that shape the collective aspects of economic activity. In other words, it is important to distinguish the overall logic of social relations from the strategies utilized by individuals and groups to find places within them or escape from them. Historically, research on regulation started from a holistic conception of social ties, although the need to specify the mediations through which individual and collective behavior are determined was not denied. In fact, it would be opportune to find the macrosocial foundations of an alternative microeconomics in a mirror image of the approach which is particularly active today and seeks to specify the microeconomic foundations of a macroeconomic theory.

The usefulness of the concept of the *mode of production* lies in specifying the links between social relations and economic organization. By this term I refer to any particular form of relations of production and exchange, that is, the social relations governing the production and reproduction of the material conditions required for human life in society. This definition is so general that it cannot be directly tested against existing societies, because it would be extremely unusual for it to be possible to represent all of the social relations making up a social formation in terms of a single, pure mode of production. Indeed, according to the Althusserian school (Terray, Rey, Balibar, Poulantzas, Fossaert), the overall structure of a given society, or its economic structure (the preferable position, which I will adopt here), is defined by a complex system of articulation of modes or production.

This distinction between "pure" modes of production and the *articulation* of a set of production and exchange relations is all the more necessary when the researcher is interested in distant eras (when, for example, the capitalist mode of production was far from dominant, even in the countries that would become the center of industrial capitalism) or in "peripheral" social formations (where a wide variety of social relations different from commodity exchange or the wage relation *stricto sensu* can be observed). Economists usually have not paid much attention to social formations termed, for want of a better label, precapitalist. However, the remarkable *convergence* between works on the regulation of capitalist economies and research by economic historians on the feudal system should be underlined. The similarities with the works of Labrousse, Kula, or Bois appear less the result of chance than the consequence of a shared methodology. They show economists how economic mechanisms vary across historical eras, helping them free themselves from their penchant for universalizing the "laws" of pure economics and considering the social forms associated with capitalism to be natural.

Keeping in mind economists' habitual object of study, I propose to limit the presentation of basic concepts here to the case in which the capitalist mode of production is dominant. As we know, the capitalist mode is characterized by the very specific form taken by the relations of exchange and production. In the first place, the exchange relation takes the commodity form. The creation of the obligation of payment in money simultaneously institutes monetary constraint and the commodity as subject. In the second place, the separation of the direct producers from their means of production and their obligation to sell their labor power define the nature of capitalist relations of production, or more generally, the nature of the wage relation. From this comes the *appearance*, for the agents on the market, that the wage relation simply duplicates the separation between commodity and producer. Actually, it introduces a social division fundamentally different from the commodity relation. This distinction is the basis for the definition of modes of production by the conjunction of the relations of production and exchange. Historical analysis, for its part, confirms that the growth

33

of commodity relations does not necessarily go along with that of wage labor. Braudel underlined the emergence of early commercial capitalism well before that of industrial capitalism.

Consequently, once industrial capitalism has been established, the workers' submission to capital is no longer merely formal, but real, so that the labor process tends to be dominated by a logic other than that of the production of use values. In fact, the wage relation affects the form of commodity exchange in turn: the primacy of exchange value over use value makes capital appear as "value creating value." Thus, the domination of the capitalist mode of production makes accumulation the essential imperative. It become a "coercive law" which imposes itself on the whole system (Lipietz 1979).

Is it possible to deduce from this principle a series of laws and tendencies that describe the inevitable, or at least probable, dynamics of the system? This would suppose a simple and reciprocal correspondence between a general form of social relations and the medium-or long-term dynamic that manifest themselves in the usual categories of economic analysis. However, the debates over historical materialism, the controversies over the tendency of the rate of profit to fall, or the problem of the transformation of value into price clearly indicate the dangers of moving too rapidly from the qualitative to the quantitative, from the esoteric to the exoteric, and more generally from one level of abstraction to another. In this respect, if accumulation does indeed constitute a tendency inherent to capitalism, it is still necessary to analyze the exact forms that it may take and the disequilibria and contradictions that they engender.

2. A First Intermediate Notion: The Regime of Accumulation

If one accepts Marx's intuitions regarding capitalism, the central question then takes the form of a paradox: how can such a contradictory process succeed over a long period of time? Indeed, if the generalization of commodity exchange makes crises possible, the conflicts stemming from the relationship of exploitation and competition between capitalists renders them more than likely—indeed, almost necessary. To the degree that the logic of capitalism is completely in command, or at least dominant, the very factors that favor profitability in the sphere of production compromise the realization process in the sphere of circulation, and thus the continuity of the process of the metamorphosis of capital itself. If, on the contrary, the reproduction of the system supposes its connection to noncapitalist modes of production, there is no automatic guarantee that the dynamics of the accumulation process will correspond to the expansion of the space in which commoditites circulate. In short, crisis, understood as a process that brutally restores the contradictory unity of the various stages of the accumulation process, ought to be the rule, not the exception.

In fact, history suggests that these contradictions can be overcome, at least partially or temporarily, so that during relatively long periods, crises of moderate intensity or even simple recessions are sufficient to reestablish a self-sustaining process of accumulation. The period subsequent to World War II illustrates such a process, which it would be difficult to interpret only as the miraculous conjunction of a series of happy accidents, to use a mirror image of the explanation of the present crisis that was offered for a time. Alternatively, one could contend that during a certain period of time, social forms may succeed in channeling and guiding the major aspects of the accumulation process, so that previous disequilibria and contradictions are *attenuated*—until their very success may reveal *new* limits to continued capital accumulation.

Studying the long-term possibilities for accumulation thus consists of searching out the different social and economic patterns involved in:

■ the evolution of the *organization of production* and of the workers' relationship to the means of production;

■ the *time horizon* for the valorization of capital, which offers a basis for the development of principles of management;

■ a *distribution of value* that allows for the reproduction and development of the different social classes or groups;

■ a composition of *social demand* that corresponds to the tendencies in the development of productive capacity; and

■ a manner of *articulation* with noncapitalist economic forms, when they hold an essential place in the economic formation under study.

From these elements comes the definition of a regime of accumulation. By this term I will designate the set of regularities that ensure the general and relatively coherent progress of capital accumulation,

35

that is, that allow for the resolution or postponement of the distortions and disequilibria to which the process continually gives rise. In fact, the five preceding characteristics appear sufficient, from a logical viewpoint, to specify the precise dynamics of growth occurring in individual sectors. This is evident for those characteristics which define the workings of the parameters necessary for putting together the equivalent of a macroeconomic model: the technical structure of a given form of production organization; the distribution of value; the composition of demand; and transfers associated with other production relations, such as rent. It is implicit as far as the time horizon for the valorization of capital is concerned. Although situated on the level of the agents' images of reality, it appears to complement a tendency toward increasingly large production organizations and the deepening of the division of labor within large-scale enterprises.

A few brief comments about the notion of regimes of accumulation are appropriate here. In the first place, the origins of the economic regularities that comprise them must in turn be explained through an analysis of the specific form of competition, of the wage relation, or of their insertion in existing international relations. In the second place, the potential for disequilibrium in the accumulation process remains, since, for example, the recurrence of more or less cyclical crises is an essential part of the adjustment process associated with any regime of accumulation (see section IV). Finally, long-term dynamic stability is not ensured, since the progressive rise and development of a regime of accumulation leads to a new form of structural crisis (see section V).

Thus, making reference to *different* regimes of accumulation enable me to avoid taking the invariant aspects of economic organization, so frequently invoked in the Marxist literature inspired by structuralism, as the alpha and omega of the analysis of a given economic formation. My central hypothesis is, in fact, that the overall reproduction of the system can take different forms. It then becomes essential to make a precise analysis of the *changes*, both qualitative and quantitative, that have been necessary for the maintenance of capitalist relations *in general* in the long run. Besides, prior research has already confirmed the variability of regimes of accumulation over time and space.

In conclusion, the imperatives and logic of accumulation can take on distinctly different forms whose consequences are by no means identical in terms of the economic dynamics and types of social organization they engender. From this emerges the usefulness of a second level of analysis which moves from social relations in general to their specific configuration in a given country and during a particular historical phase.

3. A Second Step: Defining the Exact Configuration of the Institutional Forms

The concept of structural (or institutional) forms is intended to shed light on the origins of the patterns guiding the reproduction of economic formations over given historical periods. It also extends the approach discussed above in regard to accumulation to the fundamental social relations themselves, whose invariant aspects can only be reproduced through continual alterations of their forms and precise articulations, which are particularly evident over long periods of time.

I will thus define institutional forms (or structural forms) as any kind of codfication of one or several fundamental social relations. The relevant institutional forms derive from the character of the dominant mode of production; if we limit ourselves to capitalism, three appear to be fundamental. First, there is money, which is certainly the most all-encompassing, since it defines how economic units are connected. The second is the wage relation, essential because it represents a particular kind of surplus appropriation. Finally, there is competition, which describes how units of accumulation relate to each other.

Forms of monetary constraint: How has the monetary constraint manifested itself in the successive productive systems that have appeared since the emergence of industrial capitalism? Beyond the imperative of the reproduction of the general equivalent—the basis of commodity exchange—different forms of money management are possible. I will define the specific form of the fundamental social relation that establishes the commodity subjects as the "monetary form." Theoretically speaking, money in this usage is not a particular type of commodity, but a means of establishing relations between the center of accumulation, wage earners, and other commodity subjects. Depending on whether money has a metallic or nonmaterial form, on the degree of development of the various functions that it fulfills, and on the kind of logic that dominates (private or public,

37

international or national), various types of monetary constraint can be imagined.

It is clear that the monetary form is closely related to the spaces governed by nations and those between them. On the one hand, money represents one of the key attributes of nation-states and tends to create a homogeneous space of commodity circulation within borders that are essentially political. But on the other hand, the initiatives of commodity agents or the establishment of convertibility by monetary authorities create connections with other spaces in which commodities circulate, so that monetary relations extend beyond the nation-state itself and impose limitations upon its autonomy.

This approach can be distinguished from most of the dichotomous and universalizing theories that treat inflation as a phenomenon that is essentially, if not *exclusively*, monetary and unrelated to the other organizational forms of economic activity. For one thing, money is an integral part of the reproduction of commodity systems, so their regulation is as much monetary as real. Due to this fact, the interrelated dynamics of credit and money affect the course of capital accumulation, production, and employment, not just the general price level. From this perspective, the notion of the neutrality of monetary policy, so often postulated by the monetarists (and sometimes by Marxists as well), appears invalid. Furthermore, qualitative changes in money management can imply major alterations in the dynamics of the general price level and, by extension, in all nominal incomes. This renders possible an interpretation of periods of inflation or deflation that is monetary—but not monetarist.

Configurations of the wage relation: Second, is it possible to specify different kinds of capitalist production relations? Defining different forms of the wage relation involves characterizing the mutual relations among different types of work organization, life-styles, and ways in which the labor force is reproduced. Analytically speaking, there are five components to the historically observable configurations of the capital-labor relation: the type of means of production; the social and technical division of labor; the ways in which workers are attracted and retained by the firm; the direct and indirect determinants of wage income; and lastly, the workers' way of life, which is more or less closely linked to the acquisition of commodities or the use of collective services outside the market.

Previous research on the long-run economic history of the United States and France has confirmed the existence of very different forms of the wage relation. These include the competitive form, character-ized by the limited role that workers' consumption plays in capital-ist production itself; Taylorism, in which the labor process is consid-erably reorganized, without an equivalent change in worker life-styles; and finally Fordism, which codifies a certain parallelism be-tween the development of production norms and the emergence of new consumption norms. Simply from this brief enumeration it is clear that the wage relation is connected to the different regimes of accumulation that have existed, at least in the dominant capitalist economies.

Forms of competition: Third, how are relations organized among a set of centers of accumulation who a priori make decisions inde-pendently of each other? The concept of the form of competition makes it possible to respond to this question, distinguishing various polar cases. Competitive mechanisms are at work when the fate of privately produced goods is determined by a confrontation on the market *after* production. Monopoly reigns when certain rules of socialization prevail *before* production through the maintenance of a social demand whose quantity and composition are largely geared to supply.

Of course, the distinction between a competitive stage of capital-ism and a monopolistic one is made in many analyses inspired by Marxism or institutionalism. For its part, the present approach places less emphasis on the phenomena of concentration and centralization of capital as structural characteristics and more on their implica-tions for accumulation and the dynamics of profitability. It is indeed important to explain how changes in forms of competition contrib-ute to transitions from one regime of accumulation to another. How-ever, from a theoretical viewpoint, there is nothing to ensure that these changes are the most essential elements in that process. In some cases they accompany transformations of the wage relation (Taylorism and Fordism) and the monetary constraint (the relation between monopolization and monetary credit). In others they give rise to these very transformations.

The definition of these three institutional forms leads us to a discussion of the space in which they operate, essentially the nation-state. On the one hand, the existence of a national currency estab-lishes a disjunction between the internal and external circulation of commodities. History suggests that, until now, it has always been a particular national currency—that of the hegemonic economy—that served as a basis for establishing relations between the various national economic spaces. But what explains the stability of an international monetary system and, more generally, how can each national mode of development be related to the prevailing international regime? On the other hand, the form taken by the wage relation is the result of a de facto or institutionalized compromise that is comprehensible only in terms of class alliances linked to each country's own national history. Finally, political forms historically originated in a bounded social space defined precisely by the management of the currency and of the most essential components of the wage relation. From this flows the necessity of presenting two last institutional forms which are, moreover, dialectically linked: places in the international system and the forms of the state.

Position within the international regime: The nature of a country's membership in the international regime defines a fourth social form, which is essential for the analysis of its socioeconomic dynamics. Its position is defined by the set of rules that organize the nation-state's regulations with the rest of the world, both in terms of commodity exchanges and the localization of production, via direct investment or through the financing of capital inflows and external deficits. In this regard, a quasi-autarchical accumulation process is usually juxtaposed against a national process of accumulation which would be no more than the projection within the country under consideration of a logic apparent only on a global scale. The regulation approach actually leads to a much more nuanced conception of the subject. Researchers using it have developed a series of intermediate notions which, beginning with the "international regime" (that is, the configuration of economic spaces and their connections), define the notion of the *strategic area*, the set of possibilities offered and constraints imposed by the international regime for each national space (Mistral 1986).

In this way, the dialectic between national autonomy and external constraints is put into perspective. The very characteristic of an international regime that stimulates the mode of growth of one country can inhibit or even endanger growth in another. Similarly, one should be skeptical about the internal-external dichotomy. On the one hand, national institutional forms are a response to a place in a given external configuration; on the other, conflicts and disequilibria that are internal by nature often lead to confrontations with the reigning international order for their resolution.

Thus, this approach lets us get beyond the somewhat Manichean distinction between closed and open economies made by macroeconomic theory and put into historical perspective the fashionable idea that internationalization has developed since the takeoff of industrial capitalism. In fact, the history of the past two centuries suggests that tendencies toward the globalization of capitalism and outward-looking regimes of accumulation are not characteristics of recent times only. For example, it is likely that the British economy's mode of industrialization would have been quite different in the absence of the very specific form of articulation that it enjoyed with the rest of the world. (This involved importing agricultural products and raw materials destined for industry and exporting textiles—and later machinery—mass produced in quantities exceeding the capacity of the internal market to absorb them.) Even if we limit ourselves to the contemporary era, international comparisons clearly reveal the extreme variety of places that countries occupy within the international regime, and of the specific relations that govern the internal dynamics of their economies and the tendencies of the world economy.

But beyond the question of the international position of individual countries there lies another issue: namely, the forces that ensure the cohesion of the international regime as a whole. Is it possible to define the international equivalents of national institutional forms, distinguish different principles of cohesion, and show how they have historically succeeded each other or been combined? This problem is ripe for analysis in terms of the regulation approach, with the aim of producing a theoretical construct corresponding to those obtained for regulation within nations.

Forms of the state: Relations between the state, capital, and the accumulation process have often served as the basis for periodizing various stages of the maturation of capitalism. At a more fundamental level, some theoreticians inspired by Marxism have sought to derive the state from capital, while a number of historians have analyzed its emergence through the institution of taxes and the establishment of democratic control over them. Research in terms of regulation, for its part, has not generally involved theories of the state. More modestly, it has concentrated on characterizing various forms of the state and the effects that they have on economic dynamics, the fifth key social form.

From this perspective, the state appears as the (often contradictory) totality of a set of *institutionalized compromises*, as André and Delorme (1983b) put it. Once these compromises are established, they create semiautomatic rules and regularities in the growth of public spending which, at least in principle, are radically different from the logic of commodity exchange. One might think of the differences between civil law and social security law or of those between commercial law and labor law.

In this sense, institutional forms and institutionalized compromises seem highly interdependent. On the one hand, forms of the wage relation and competition affect the management of transfer payments and public expenditures for economic purposes. On the other, laws, regulations, and rules imposed or confirmed by the state often play an essential role in spreading, and sometimes even originating, essential institutional forms. This is the case for the management of the collective costs associated with the labor force and for the codification of certain rules governing competition (industrial regulation, the tax system, government purchases, etc.). Taking into account the number and complexity of the links between state intervention and economic activity, it is not surprising that it has been possible to associate transitions from one regime of accumulation to another with changes in the form of the state. Whether narrowly circumscribed or part of a broader system, the state plays a definite role in the establishment, rise, and crisis of every regime of accumulation.

Consequently, the state cannot be defined without reference to the economic system, although it is not necessary to adopt a strictly functionalist conception of its interventions in order to do this. Thus, an economic policy may initially prove highly successful but later prove incapable of copying with disequilibria that grow from local and limited to general and cumulative. According to this conception of the forms of state intervention, neither strict predetermination nor complete autonomy is the rule.

4. From Partial Patterns to Overall Regulation

Some of the institutional forms presented above (the wage relation, competition, and position in the international regime) help determine the prevailing regime of accumulation. However, the latter is defined only at the level of the whole economic system, with a certain degree of abstraction. Of course, once the dynamic stability of the system has been confirmed, time after time the principles governing accumulation end up intuitively *internalized* by economic agents and groups, though always imperfectly and incompletely. But it remains to be explained how these agents and groups manage collectively to adjust their decisions on a day-to-day basis, knowing only the constraints they face *locally* and not the "immanent laws" governing the whole economy.

The search for a definition: Moving from a set of bounded rationalities involved in many decentralized decisions about production and exchange to the possibility of maintaining the dynamic coherence of the whole economic system is exactly the point of the regulation approach. On the one hand, contrary to the claims of traditional equilibrium theories, convergence toward a static equilibrium is highly unlikely in the conditions in which real economies operate. Overall adjustments in production, social demand, the distribution of income, and financial flows result from the interaction of mechanisms that are partial, imperfect, and slow. They lack the complete consistency that the concept of general equilibrium supposes. On the other hand, according to recent research (Akerlof 1984, among others), the internal logic of institutions, forms of organization within the enterprise, and the labor contract, etc., have the effect of inducing adjustments *fundamentally* different from those occurring in perfectly competitive pure markets. They do not constitute mere temporary aberrations or local curiosities, reflecting the irreducible distance between theoretical representations and the complexity of real historical phenomena, but rather stable configurations of social relations, which ensure the long-term reproduction of the socioeconomic years.

I will therefore use the term *mode of regulation* to designate any set of procedures and individual and collective behaviors that serve to:

- *reproduce fundamental social relations* through the combination of historically determined institutional forms;

- *support and "steer" the prevailing regime of accumulation;* and

- ensure the compatibility over time of a *set of decentralized decisions,* without the economic actors themselves having to internalize the adjustment principles governing the overall system.

It is evident that this notion is intended to substitute for the theory of individual choice and the concept of general equilibrium as starting points for the study of macroeconomic phenomena. In effect, every mode of regulation describes how the existing combination of institutional forms fashions, guides, and in certain cases constrains individual behavior. It also predetermines the workings of adjustment mechanisms operating through the market, which usually derive from a set of rules and organizational principles without which they could not function. In this conception, it is impossible to establish a dichotomy between the purely economic on one side and the social on the other. Even perfectly competitive pure markets derive from the organization of social space; they are constructed on the basis of power relations and legal rules.

Of course, neither a certain degree of autonomy of individual strategy nor the diversity of behavior within a given set of institutional forms can be denied. But in summary form, one might say that struggles to attain some classification within a given hierarchy cannot be assimilated to class struggles or, more exactly, to confrontations in which the stakes involve the overthrow of the existing power relations and rules of the game.

How do institutional forms work? This, in fact, is the central question, if one wants to go from simply noting patterns to explaining their logic and genesis—or to trying to change them. Work within the regulation school on this very ambitious question is only at its beginnings, seeking initial hypotheses and intuitions that could serve as bases for later formulations. Very schematically, it is possible to suggest three ways in which institutional forms act.

1. *Laws, rules,* and *regulations,* initially defined at the collective level, are intended to impose certain types of economic behavior on groups and individuals through coercion (whether direct or symbolic and mediated). Yet constraint cannot be considered the only principle underlying economic and social patterns. First of all, in democratic societies, laws must be passed and enjoy at least a minimum of acquiescence among political representatives. Second, and above all, if the law comes into conflict with existing power relations, or if it excessively contradicts the logic of private interests (particularly economic ones), it is circumvented. Losing all meaning, it falls into desuetude due to the divorce that occurs between the individual and the collectivity. This, in turn, suggests a second way in which institutional forms operate.

2. Reaching a *compromise,* after negotiations, represents a mode of action different a priori from the preceding one. Private agents or groups arrive at certain conventions which govern their mutual engagements on the basis of their own interests. If money undoubtedly

constitutes the archetype of a collective institution, wage agreements resulting from labor-management negotiations provide a good example of this second form. Besides, the two are not mutually exclusive, since a private accord (for example, a collective bargaining agreement) can be extended by law or regulation to groups beyond the parties initially concerned (for example, in French labor law a contract can be extended over the whole of an industry). This process of transmutation from the individual to the collective is quite prevalent in various types of law, including labor, commercial, and even administrative law.

3. There also exists a third means of establishing an implicit code and relatively homogeneous behavior. Even in the absence of laws or private agreements, the existence of a common *value system,* or at least of common *representations of reality,* may be sufficient to ensure that routine replaces the diversity and spontaneity of individual impulses and initiatives. Such is the case for religious beliefs and rules of good conduct. In the economic sphere, the same is true with respect to long-term expectations (the views concerning the future dear to Keynes) and images of the workings of the economy and the rules of the game in the society under consideration. Thus, depending on the case, the same social relation may derive either from binding legal rules or from an implicit common system of representations. In the event of the latter, acceptance of the prevailing norms appears to be the expression of individuals' free will. Within such a framework, new social relations may also be established in the guise of the old rules, whose effects are actually transformed. As examples, one might think of the peculiarities of the wage relation in Japan or of the generalization of agricultural wage labor in the guise of traditional production relations in certain Latin American countries.

These remarks bring us to a discussion of the relationship between the present approach and approaches based upon the concept of equilibrium. There is a considerable difference between my position and the way the concept of general equilibrium is used (sometimes dogmatically) by neoclassical thinkers. In fact, in the long sweep of history, just as in contemporary economies, preferences and productive possibilities are not defined a priori, but themselves result from socioeconomic processes. Therefore, it would not be possible to define an equilibrium independently of the social framework that determines it. It then becomes difficult to regard crises as instances of the inadequacy of social forms in relation to a supposedly unique, preexisting equilibrium.

But the divergences are fewer between the regulation approach and some recent research which, though neoclassical in method, has been unorthodox in its object: the origins and stability of representations, institutions, and agreements. I will briefly note three directions that this research has taken.

1. Substituting the criterion of *bounded rationality* for that of global rationality, Simon (1982) proposed suggestive models of organizations and the choice procedures that economic agents use to deal with the information pertinent to them. He was one of the first to specify the differences between a contract for the offer of services and a labor contract, noting some of the determinants that condition this choice. It is significant that the wage relation appears as an alternative to the commodity relation, and that it seems superior to it. This is one of the first examples of an explanation of an institution as the expression of a rationality superior to that of the market.

2. Likewise, the *theory of repetitive games* suggests some interesting intuitions concerning the roles of institutions and conventions. Aren't they the means of avoiding the persistence of the prisoner's dilemma over time? In Schotter (1981) one can find an effort not to take organizational forms as exogenous givens—in a sense, as parasites—but rather as constituent elements of a certain stability and optimality in socioeconomic processes.

3. Finally, we can thank some economic theoreticians and mathematical economists for demonstrating that the general equilibrium method could take anticipations, value systems, cognitive processes, and noncommodity relations into account. The originality of the models elaborated by researchers like Akerlof (1984) lies in showing that there may (or may not) exist as many equilibria as there are sociocultural systems that condition economic choices. His formalizations of societies organized on the basis of castes, customs, and beliefs that appear "irrational" a priori, along with his formalizations of labor contracts, illustrate convincingly the possibility of reversing the economist's approach to the social sphere.

It is nonetheless appropriate to note an important difference between this "enlightened neoclassicism" and the regulation approaches. Collective action is not necessarily the product of the aggregation and coalescence of atomized individuals whose behavior is a priori independent. Beyond that, the interpretation I have given to the preceding models is not always that of their authors. In conformity with their epistemological and methodological postulates, the neoclassicists tend to want to set out the abstract logical foundations of institutions in all times and places. In so doing, they fail to see another question that, however, is essential for any long-term historical research. In what circumstances do organizational forms develop and come to define a stable system of economic adjustment, or, on the contrary, decline and go into crisis?

The concept of regulation used here is not that of the other sciences. The preceding chapter has already underlined the semantic ambiguity of the term "regulation." Paradoxically, the idea was introduced to economics by the classical authors, who were seeking a concept of equilibrium or at least of equilibration. Much more recently, works by Destanne de Bernis and by the GRREC have referred to the definition of regulation used by physics, biology, and systems theory, or else to Canguilhem's very general formulation cited above (p. 15). However, these connections can lead to unfortunate misunderstandings, because the way the notion can be used in the social sciences (and in which it has in fact been elaborated by the regulation school) is different.

In the first place, the scientists' insistence on *the role of rules and norms* must be put into perspective. Adhesion to a common set of moral, legal, or economic norms constitutes only one of the three principles that define institutional forms. Constraint (whether private or state) and contract (individual or collective) represent the two others.

In the second place, it is not certain that in economic life actions are "initially distinct" from each other. In fact, starting from the places that individuals occupy within a system of social relations prevents us from conceiving of the cohesion of a society as the happy but accidental result of a series of individual acts that are a priori distinct. Every institutional form generalizes at least a partial principle of socialization, and makes possible transitions from the macro level to the micro level. Consequently, the cohesion of the socioeconomic system is not the simple effect of self-correcting loops on the factors making for destabilization, in what would be the equivalent of a vast, complex social machine.

Moreover—and this is the third difference—no actor or group plays the role of the *systems engineer*, ensuring the dynamic stability of the economy through conscious and deliberate action. The break with the Keynesian conception of the state and economic policy is significant. The tangled connections between institutionalized compromises, whose consequences are sometimes contradictory, render impossible a strictly functionalist view of state intervention. Likewise, and contrary to what the term "regulation" implies, this approach is much less functionalist than are many simplifications of Marxist theory. The state is not a priori a prop for monopoly capital, nor is it the vector of a silent but ineluctable transition to socialism.

One should be extremely suspicious of teleological interpretations of the type, "In order to survive, the system needed Keynesian state, a Fordist wage relation," and so on. At the most, one can conclude that the wage relation and state form, *once constituted*, were compatible with *one* viable mode of development, because others could a priori have been envisaged. Likewise, this approach breaks with the Marxist tradition which makes capital into an omniscient and sometimes Machiavellian collective subject, managing the contradictions it engenders at will. To begin with, the periodization of regimes of accumulation and of modes of regulation does not correspond to those that underline the inevitable succession of competitive capitalism, monopoly, and state monopoly capitalism. Furthermore, it is difficult to specify a general law governing the evolution of the system as soon as one rejects the seductive but fallacious hypothesis that social relations will always ultimately adapt themselves to the categorical imperative represented by the growth of the productive forces.

The objective of the regulation school is both different and more modest. It is to explain the rise and subsequent crises of *modes of development* (that is, combinations of a regime of accumulation and a type of regulation), leaving the question of the long-run tendencies of capitalism open until enough historical studies and international comparisons have accumulated. Finally, it should not be forgotten that every regime of accumulation is characterized by the particular forms that economic disequilibria and social conflicts take within it. As a result, crises do not result from mere functional maladjustments, but reflect the effects of social structure on interrelated short-term behaviors. The subsequent course of the crisis leads to a much more open-ended process of *transition* between the old regime and a new mode of development, which remains uncertain and fragile.

iv. LEVELS AND KINDS OF CRISES: A TYPOLOGY

The literature on economic crises offers a variety of distinctly different analyses of their origins, their development, and even whether they are accidental or necessary in nature. At one end of the theoretical spectrum, the vast majority of neoclassical models do not have a place for the concept of crisis. At most, they use the term for a corrective phase following a boom, whose duration is due to the length or imperfection of the adjustment processes. Moreover, they hold that the factors that either initiate a period of growth or precipitate a downturn are usually unpredictable shocks. At the other extreme, some reductionist and rather deterministic Marxist analyses hold that capitalist economies are by nature subject to various aspects of a structural crisis, now latent, soon to be open, which will eventually lead to the collapse of the mode of production itself. Between the caprices of chance and the iron law of inevitable decline, it would seem that there is room for a number of definitions and levels of crises.

1. Crises as "External" Disturbances

In this first sense, crises are defined as episodes during which the continued *economic reproduction* of a given geographic entity is *blocked*, either due to shortages linked to natural or climatic disasters, or to an economic collapse originating in external events or wars. The peculiarity of this type of crisis is that it results neither from the normal workings of the mode of regulation (see section 2) below nor from the exhaustion of that mode (see section 3) or of the regime of accumulation (see section 4). Nevertheless, the type of regulation in existence determines the forms that the contraction of economic activity and the dynamics of prices and incomes will take in response to these "external" causes of crisis.

It is thus a tradition among specialists in the economic history of feudalism to underline the role of climatic fluctuations in determining whether harvests were good or bad. Their effects can be shown on industry and commerce, and thus on the rest of the economy. Likewise, successive shortages of raw materials (the cotton crisis) and speculative "bubbles" are frequently (though perhaps more debatably) invoked to explain short-term economic fluctuations during the nineteenth century. Finally, at one time, economists interpreted events after 1973 as essentially the consequence of a series of increases in raw material prices—"oil shocks," "dollar shocks," etc. One might think of the McCracken report to the OECD in this connection, even if it also pointed to more structural factors.

49

Without denying the role of chance and the accidental, one legitimately might be skeptical about an analytic framework that allows only for this type of crisis. How can it be that shocks that a priori are contingent produce recurrent periods of growth followed by depression? Why doesn't the same accident produce the same effects over time? (In our day, an agricultural crisis means a *shortage* in the poorest countries, but massive *surpluses* in the United States or the European Economic Community.) Finally, is treating the discontinuities of the 1970s as merely the consequence of the "exceptional conjunction of a series of unfortunate accidents" really a sound way to explain phenomena so general, durable, and significant? These questions offer a basis for other definitions of the notion of crisis. Even in the absence of exogenous shocks, isn't crisis a necessary phase in the long-term reproduction of capitalist systems?

2. Cyclical Crises: An Integral Part of the Regulation of a Stable Mode of Development

In this second view, crises are held to correspond to the phase in which tensions and disequilibria accumulated during periods of expansion are wiped out. They take place within the existing economic mechanisms and social patterns, and thus within the prevailing mode of regulation in a given country and era. In this sense, the recurrence of phases favorable and unfavorable for accumulation is the direct consequence of the reigning institutional forms, which cyclical crises affect only very slowly and partially. They may indeed induce an acceleration of financial concentration and centralization, but without changing the prevailing form of competition. Likewise, they may restore "labor discipline" and the necessary distribution of income without affecting the dominant form of the wage relation. In contrast with the first definition, in this case one can speak of *totally endogenous* crises, that is, crises that occur from time to time without unpredictable shocks.

It was undoubtedly Marx's merit to have been the first to perceive the novelty of this phenomenon specific to capitalism and to have proposed theories to account for it. In their way, the theories of business cycles have detailed and formalized different explanations of the origins of economic crises: insufficient demand, sectoral or sectional distortions, the decline of the rate of profit due to a distribution of income that has become more favorable to workers, or financial instability and limits to credit expansion. Even if the models differ according to the emphasis placed on one or another factor, they all engender an automatic switch from boom to crisis, then from stagnation to renewed growth. The latter occurs when excess capacity has been adjusted to match existing sales opportunities and complementarity among sectors restored through the cessation of activity by some producers, the entry of new ones, changes in the rate of profit, and shifts in investment. Efforts to increase productivity and pressure on the workers bring the rate of profit back up and favor renewed accumulation and improved expectations concerning the future. Finally, the reestablishment of consistency in the returns to capital in its two forms (industrial and financial) and the restoration of financial health through the effects of monetary constraint furnish a basis for the renewed expansion of investment.

It remains the case that *the depth and form of cyclical crises depend on the characteristics of the prevailing type of regulation,* as both historical and theoretical research have shown. In the context of the monopolistic system of regulation that was progressively established in the dominant countries after World War II, depressions (in the strict sense of an absolute decline in production) were superceded by simple recessions. Economists eventually were able to ask seriously whether the business cycle had not become obsolete, thanks to the accuracy of economic forecasting, the efficacy of countercyclical policies, and the precision of economic theory! The experience of the past decade shows how much these views erred on the side of optimism. Even after the influence of the oil price increases diminished with the oil price decline and America's renewed growth from late 1982 on stimulated international trade, by the mid-1980s few countries had returned to their growth rates of the 1960s. Is this not an indication that the adjustments now underway are not self-correcting, and that they reflect the destabilization of the previous system of regulation?

An affirmative response to this question would lead us to define, in contrast to the second type of crisis, *structural crises* or "great crises." I will use these terms for any period in which economic and social dynamics come into contradiction with the mode of development that drives them or, in other words, in which the contradictory character of the long-term reproduction of the system becomes apparent. The historical precedents (the long depression of the end of the nineteenth century, the collapse of 1929) suggest that the great crisis ultimately affects the mode of regulation as well as the regime

51

of accumulation. From an analytic viewpoint it is, however, important to distinguish two major types of structural crises, depending
on whether it is the system of regulation that destabilizes the regime
of accumulation (see section 3), or the latter that undermines the
mode of regulation (see section 4).

3. Crises of the System of Regulation

An episode in which the mechanisms associated with the prevailing
mode of regulation prove incapable of overcoming unfavorable short-
term tendencies, even though the regime of accumulation was at
least *initially* viable, will be defined as a crisis of the system of
regulation. If I go a bit further in this analysis, three circumstances
that may lead to such a failure can be distinguished:

■ *External or internal disturbances of a new type* that cannot
be brought under control within a system of regulation whose
structural stability, progressively established over time, is
founded upon responses to other types of problems. This type
of crisis is in a sense complementary to that defined above
(crises as external disturbances). The essential factor is less the
intensity of the exogenous shock than its incompatibility with
the economic formation under consideration—or the inadequacy of the latter.

■ *Sociopolitical struggles* threatening existing institutional
compromises, or situations where the conjunction of individual strategies destroys components of the overall mode of regulation, so that the social structure becomes incompatible with
the enlarged reproduction of the economic system. The crisis
then reflects conflicts between the rates of political and economic change.

■ On the other hand, the *logical development of the established system of regulation* can lead to the exhaustion of the
sources of growth and the beginnings of long-term crisis. In
this case, depression results less from the inadequacy and im-
maturity of the regulatory system than from its full *maturity.*
In a way, past successes contribute to the origins of present
crisis, and perhaps to its outbreak and precise form as well.
Even if chance and unexpected events do play an obvious role

in the crisis of a system of regulation, one could not simply reduce it to a "giant fluctuation" or a disturbance of a new type. It is thus important to distinguish the factors that spark a crisis from those that propagate it. A system of regulation goes into crisis when local disequilibria combine and can no longer be handled by the socioeconomic procedures in force.

These three types of crisis within a regulatory system may themselves stem from any of its components: the inadequacy of existing forms of competition, the wage relation, state intervention, monetary management, or a country's position in international relations. To cast some light on the preceding definition, it may be useful to classify some of the interpretations that have been proposed in the literature for the crisis of 1929 and that of today.

The Roots of the Crisis of 1929 Differed from Those of Today's

Without considering the validity of the various theories that have been offered, it should be noted that the hypothesis of a crisis of the system of regulation is frequently advanced to explain the interwar crisis, even if each author places the accent on one particular component. Thus the transition from competitive to monopoly capitalism is said to have induced an alteration in the fundamental law of the equalization of rates of profit, and to have produced sectoral disproportions which led to the crisis (Borelly 1975; Destanne de Bernis 1977). Likewise, the American administered pricing school holds that changes in the forms of competition were responsible for accentuating disequilibria between excess production capacity and inadequate demand, due to excess profits and distortions of relative prices (Berle and Means 1933). At a more fundamental level, the theory of imperfect competition seems to accompany this development in industrial structure (Chamberlain 1933; Sweezy 1939; Robinson 1943).

A second broad category of theories underlines the inadequacies of the mechanisms for *wage determination*. Due to the persistence of a competitive logic in this area, the boom of the 1920s benefited employment and real wages very little, so that the Great Depression represented a "forced" redistribution of productivity gains to wage earners (Ozanne, and in a certain sense, Baran and Sweezy 1966). This is similar to the analyses that regard the inadequacy of the wage relation vis-à-vis the unprecedented growth of Taylorism as one of the key factors behind the crisis of 1929 (Aglietta 1976; Boyer 1979).

Monetarists and Keynesians, for their part, agree that the conduct of *economic policy* was an essential cause of the crisis of 1929, even if they differ about which precise factor was responsible. For the former, the ill-considered laxity of the monetary authorities, followed by their excessive rigor, would explain the snowballing and depth of the Depression (Friedman and Schwartz 1963; contested by Temin 1976). In their view, the crisis did not emerge from the private sphere of regulation, but from governmental intervention, which is destabilizing by nature. The Keynesians' analysis is based on the opposite hypothesis. Principally for ideological reasons, conservative governments would not allow themselves to follow countercyclical policies and launch public spending programs, which only the state is capable of carrying out, to pull the economy out of the rut of underemployment and reverse unfavorable expectations (Keynes 1936; Robinson 1943).

Finally, the *failure of adjustment mechanisms at the international level* represents a fourth possible cause of the crisis. The complete incoherence of the financial flows created by the Treaty of Versailles was reinforced by the decline of British hegemony and the United States' reluctance to act as the dominant power that stabilizes international economic relations was manifested in the variety, and in many cases the radicalism, of the solutions that were attempted (import restrictions, protectionism, competitive devaluations).

Appropriately amended, analyses of the current crisis stress an analogous set of factors, even if most of the institutional forms and partial systems of regulation are now working the other way around. If the spread of monopolistic competition favored growth and deadened economic fluctuations after World War II, various structural changes have called this virtuous circle into question. The aging of basic industries, the tapering off of demand for consumer durables, and the rise of new industries and more flexible methods of production have together destabilized the previous forms of competition. In turn, this change has affected the distribution of profits and the dynamics of investment.

Likewise, Fordist wage relations have fallen into crisis from the effects of pressures that varied country by country: worker struggles challenging the organization of work, wage demands not matched by productivity increases, or socialization by the state of a growing share of the collective costs associated with the industrial urban lifestyle. More generally, the codification of various forms of rights to income, independent of one's economic situation, has become a source of both economic and sociopolitical tension as increases in productivity have slowed.

The same limits may apply to the growth of public spending and regulatory activity: easily accepted by society while it enjoyed "the dividends of growth," they provoked taxpayer revolt when the postwar growth process became blocked and gave rise to a host of mutually canceling transfers. This situation is sometimes analyzed theoretically as a zero-sum game (Thurow 1975). Likewise, the limits of the existing rules governing money and credit management became apparent: in the absence of a restoration of profit rates to previous levels, the credit system socialized the losses, often through inflation. An analogous mechanism began to operate with respect to public spending: no longer countercyclical, government borrowing became cumulative, so that the medium-term viability of fiscal policy became doubtful. Whether rightly or wrongly, the ideologues of the minimal state and the "return to the market" exploit these chinks in the principles of Keynesianism, which represented a major component of the postwar mode of regulation.

The steady disintegration of the hierarchy that stabilized international relations is just as evident. A system conceived to work on the basis of a large U.S. trade surplus and a stable exchange rate for the dollar broke down as the economic and industrial hegemony of the United States weakened. The conflicts between the internal and external roles of the dollar worsened, to the point where they affected international investment flows and commerce. The absence of a system that could ensure the coherent functioning of structurally fragmented national economies then became patent. This is what led numerous authors to speak of the crisis of regulation in the international economy and the absence of a national system of regulation (Michalet, Mabeuf, and Ominami 1984) or of the contradiction between systems of regulation still operating on a national basis and the forces operating on a global scale (Destanne de Bernis 1977, 1983a).

This list of factors making for crisis gives rise to two questions. In the first place, how can the combined effects of these different sources of disequilibrium be analyzed? Can we be sure that they do not compensate for each other and that, on the contrary, they have touched off a *cumulative* process that is breaking down the previously existing patterns? I will detail below the different methods through which this may be done. They include tests of the stability of a macroeconomic model that represents the prevailing system of regulation, and qualitative analyses of the changes occurring in its institutional forms. In the second place, when crises of regulation have gone beyond a certain threshold, don't they risk provoking a crisis of the *whole mode of development?* Or, in certain cases, wouldn't it be the contradictions of the regime of accumulation itself that make themselves felt within the system of regulation? These possibilities lead me to define a fourth type of crisis.

4. A Higher Stage of Crisis: Crises of the Mode of Development

In contrast to the preceding sort of crisis, this type is defined by the attainment of the limits of the most essential institutional forms—those that shape the regime of accumulation—and the rise of contradictions within them. It implies in due time the crisis of the system of regulation, and thus of the whole mode of development. During such an episode, the most essential economic patterns come into question: those underlying the organization of production, the time horizon for the valorization of capital, the distribution of value, and the composition of social demand.

In qualitative terms, one could say that this type of crisis is more serious that the preceding ones because it is no longer a question of a temporary, partial disequilibrium in the mechanisms of regulation, but rather of the blockage of the process of dynamic reproduction of the economy under consideration (Billaudot 1976). However, the difficulty is that, in practice, the institutional forms underlying the regime of accumulation are also involved in the mode of regulation, so that it is difficult to distinguish clearly between these two types of crises. To those living through it, a crisis of the mode of development can take on the appearance of a simple maladjustment of one aspect of the regulatory system—economic policy, for instance. Only the deepening of the crisis and its consequent long duration will render credible the hypothesis of a crisis of the mode of development or, to use the terminology noted above, a great crisis (Boyer 1979). To the historian, looking back with hindsight, the diagnosis appears much easier, because the break that occurred can be noted in the differences existing in the subsequent phase of renewed growth, which is characterized by a different mode of development. Of course, this does not bar the recognition of a crisis of development earlier on, almost in "real time." In terms of my approach, three criteria allow us to define such an occurrence.

1. The continuation of previous patterns *does not allow the automatic reestablishment of the rate of profit,* and thus an endogenous renewal of accumulation. Due to this fact, short-run economic patterns differ fundamentally from those of the preceding period of growth (Bowles, Gordon, and Weisskopf 1983), so that the hypothesis of a descending Kondratiev wave combined with a Juglar cycle takes shape (see Schumpeter's analysis of 1929).

2. More fundamentally, *the dynamics of accumulation undermine and destroy the social forms* that supported the process during the period of growth. Subsequently, the decline of the old production methods and the exhaustion of demand for the corresponding products are accompanied by a search for alternative forms, along with new products, technologies, and plant locations. The most surprising thing is that very different—indeed, opposing—solutions are sought in hopes of overcoming the *same limits* to a crisis-stricken mode of accumulation. Although they operate within a different framework, in this my views are similar to the neo-Schumpeterian thinkers who underline the breakdown of the relationship between technical innovation and institutional change (Perez 1981).

3. Due to this fact, *the appearance of a strict economic or technological determinism ceases to prevail.* Since past compromises and behavioral rules are no longer able to ensure the economic and social consistency of the system's elements, various struggles—open or latent, offensive and/or defensive, based on innovative ideas or atavistic temptations—take place around attempts to impose different "rules of the game" (which may be new practices or old ones reestablished), exploiting the characteristics of the immediate conjuncture. It is this last criterion that is patently different from Kondratiev-type approaches. On the one hand, there is no automatic mechanism ensuring the passage from a descending phase B to an ascending phase A, unlike that which occurs at the apex of the cycle. On the other, there is no historical law that enables us to foresee what the components of the eventual new regime of accumulation in gestation will be, once we have renounced the concept of determination, in the last instance, of social relations by the productive forces.

Earlier research on the United States and France (Aglietta 1976; CEPREMAP-CORDES 1977), Europe (Boyer 1986a), and the countries of the Third World (Ominami 1986; Hausmann 1981) has shown that one could operationalize the notion of a crisis of the mode of development. Moreover, there are as many forms of this type of crisis as there are regimes of accumulation. One would be the blockage of the regime by the elimination of the working population at a more rapid rate than it enters industrial employment under an extensive system of accumulation in the crisis of 1848. Another would be cumulative collapse during the transition to an intensive regime, due to the limits inherent to autoaccumulation in sector I of the economy and obstacles to the growth of demand in sector II as in the crisis of 1929. When this is recognized, it is not surprising that the intensive regime of accumulation based upon mass consumption has come up against contradictions that, initially at least, are different. These include unfavorable changes in the rate of profit due to the intensification of Fordism, struggles concerning the distribution of income, and the consequences of increasingly rapid obsolesence for the disparity between gross and net profitability.

The four levels of crisis defined above implicitly suppose a certain *plasticity* in capitalist social relations, a capacity for change in their precise forms, so that this mode of production has until now been able to overcome a series of major crises and dramatic occurrences, such as the two world wars. To paraphrase a famous proverb, must not "things change more, to stay essentially the same"? Is it therefore necessary to conclude that capitalism will endure forever? Since there is no theoretical basis for this conclusion, a fifth and final level of crisis must be defined.

5. The Final Crisis of a Dominant Mode of Production

By the term "final crisis" I designate the *collapse of the specific set of social relations* that characterizes a mode of production. In other words, such a crisis occurs when an economic formation reaches the limits of *one* arrangement of institutional forms, precipitating challenges to and the abolition of the most *fundamental* aspects of the prevailing set of social relations. In a sense, this definition resembles the concept of "organic crisis" in orthodox Marxist theory. But it adds certain specifications and requirements that prevent us from turning every crisis, even simple short-term ones, into the final crisis of the capitalist mode of production.

In a purely *retrospective* analysis, concerning, for example, feudalism, it is possible to recognize this fifth level of crisis unambiguously. First of all, this can be done by showing how the laws regarding the tendencies of the system bore within them the germ of the crisis—specifically, the shrinkage of surplus. Second, it is possible to specify the factors and events that made this tendency into a reality. Finally, we can observe radical sociopolitical change, which impelled the overthrow of the existing relations of production and exchange in law and in actual practice. The works of Ernest Labrousse (and more recently, those of Bois) illustrate such an approach.

The question is much more complex when it is posed *prospectively,* during a capitalist crisis of one of the four preceding types. How can we be sure that the present limits of the institutional forms constitute an irresolvable blockage of the mechanisms of the mode of production? When this occurs, it is not sufficient to offer an abstract demonstration of the contradictory nature of capitalism *in general,* but rather to show that these contradictions can no longer be overcome, even temporarily, by modifications in the existing institutional forms or by the emergence of new ones. At the risk of surrendering to a determinism that is surely excessive, the demonstration of this impossibility must occur at two levels:

1. The analyst must first try to show that no possible reorganization of social relations could lead to a viable mode of development. But the task is not an easy one, since a theoretical approach that attempts to explore all the possible combinations (analogous to that of Fossaert) is beyond the capabilities of the analyst. Furthermore, one would risk concluding that certain types of reorganization were theoretically possible, when they might not have the slightest chance of actually coming into existence, given the existing sociopolitical relations and economic linkages. Such a criterion is thus difficult to operationalize, and certainly fallacious. Therefore, a second, more restrictive definition appears necessary.

2. The observer can attempt to show that in all probability, the likely tendencies in the evolution of the society, along with the nature of sociopolitical conflict, bar a reorganization of the institutional forms that would lead to a new regime of accumulation. The problem is that the analyst must then combine the faculties of a Leonardo da Vinci of the social sciences (sociologist, political scien-

tist, economist, military strategist, etc.) in a subtle mixture, while avoiding the traps of subjectivity and the received ideas that people hold as products of their time! However, the precedents offered by the greatest thinkers—whether Marxist or not—clearly show how difficult "the concrete analysis of a concrete situation" really is. Thus, in the mid-1980s, this objective seems rather unattainable, and far from the pressing questions of the day.

No doubt the reader may find this fifth type of crisis, the subject of long-standing controversy among Marxists, simply irrelevant. Nevertheless, from a methodological viewpoint, it is interesting to sketch in its outlines. On the one hand, it illustrates the connections between concepts going from the mode of regulation to the mode of production, moving in the opposite direction from the exposition in section 3 of this chapter. On the other, it was not so long ago that some Marxists saw the beginning of the collapse of capitalism and the arrival of socialism in a downturn in U.S. auto production!

This is precisely the sort of telescoping of different levels of analysis that the regulation approach seeks to avoid by setting out a series of precise, operationalized definitions of crises. (In this regard, appendix 2 summarizes the different concepts introduced above.)

v. ON METHOD: HOW CAN THESE CONCEPTS BE PUT TO USE?

As the reader has surely noticed, until now I have only discussed general concepts and their relationships with each other. Strictly speaking, I have presented more of a *general approach* than a complete theory, much less a model directly testable against empirical reality. So now I must explain how these notions can be applied in research work on a specific topic (this or that social formation or structural form studied over the long term). Ultimately, the definitions are less important in themselves than for the way in which they assist research, since their worth can only be shown by techniques that allow the verification of their adequacy as descriptions of the long-term dynamics of capitalist economies. Broadly speaking, I might call my proposed method a well-tempered Cartesianism. It has four main steps.

1. Using History to Establish a Periodization of Institutional Forms

The attention the members of the regulation school have given to changes in the forms of social relations, and the questions they have posed about their cohesion in a system—which may be viable or in crisis—can guide a reading of works by historians on the working-class movement and the labor force, the bourgeoisie and industriali-zation, the bureaucracy and the state, diplomacy and international relations, etc. On this basis, the economist can seek the *key dates* that mark significant changes in the institutional domain, involving the form of competition, the wage relation, the state-society rela-tion, and the nation-state's position in international relations. The idea is to contrast *two phases:* that in which the social relations display continuity and fall within the logic of the existing forms, and that in which, on the contrary, the stakes are precisely the constitu-tion of new institutional forms.

But the analysis cannot be exclusively qualitative. Even at this stage, it is important to specify whether the corresponding form is embryonic, limited but growing rapidly, or dominant and declining. A minimum of quantification appears necessary, whether it con-cerns the concentration or centralization of capital, the relative size of the labor force, the composition of the commodities that are part of the workers' life-style, the growth of transfer payments and public spending, or the size of the geographic zone over which exchange, production, and accumulation are organized.

The combination of these two kinds of analysis can then suggest a partial periodization for each of the institutional forms. It should be pointed out, however, that such a periodization deals with the *long run.* In particular, it is not concerned with the minor changes continually occuring in forms of economic organization. It is in this that the regulation approach distinguishes itself from a mere recapi-tulation of events or a vague institutionalism.

Finally, and above all, the results obtained cannot be extrapolated from one economic formation to another, even if they are similar. In this regard, one should examine work concerning the transforma-tions of the wage relation in Europe after 1945 (Grando, Margirier, and Buffieux 1980) and after 1973 (Boyer 1986a), the role of the state (André and Delorme 1983a), or of international position and compet-itiveness (Mistral 1986; Barou and Keiser 1984; CEPII 1983, 1984, 1986; Boyer and Ralle 1986). These differentiations take on an even greater importance when we move on to the dominated economic formations, as the works of Ominami (1980, 1986), Hausmann (1981), and Aboites (1986) bear witness.

2. Begin with the Implicit Logic of Each Institutional Form and Confirm Its Domain of Applicability

It is, in fact, rather difficult to postulate a universal principle of rationality once one has recognized the diversity of the social relations and adjustment principles that determine the behavior of economic actors and partial systems of regulation. Far from judging institutions by the standard of an immanent rationality, economists need to take note of the state of social relations and economic structures in their theoretical representations. Their task is then to deduce the form taken within them by rationalities that are always partial. The latter lie at the origin of the rules and regularities prevailing in the economic order. Although they contradict the pure model of *homo economicus*, as well as that of general equilibrium, they nonetheless have a certain consistency, and therefore a degree of permanence, once historically established.

From that point on, the question is no longer studying failures to realize the ideal of competition, but rather characterizing the various logics concerning the determination of incomes, overall demand, and even prices. Taking mechanisms for wage determination as an example, one can specify three distinct possibilities. One is Old Regime–type regulation, involving cyclical crises of rocketing prices, shrinking employment, and declining real wages, in which demographic adjustments (birth, death, and marriage rates) play an essential role. Competitive regulation seems to make labor power a commodity like any other, whose price is determined less by preestablished norms than by the short-run economic situation, the strengths of each participant's local market position, and the qualifications required for particular types of work. In this regard, some economic historians have suggested that wages are determined by fluctuations in economic activity, and not just the unemployment rate (Rougerie 1968). Their results suggest the possibility of formulating new analyses of wage determination different from the traditional Phillips curve, and show the distance between the model of pure, perfect competition and the regulation approach. In contrast, "administered" or monopolistic regulation provides for steady increases in wage income through a sort of de facto indexation, partly as a function of consumer prices, and partly in terms of productivity trends.

Here, econometric tests can enable us to determine the extent to which the statistical data concerning the different historical periods conform to these idealized models. They allow the pursuit of two possible lines of investigation. If one looks at the data on a sector-by-sector (or country-by-country) basis, how are the different ideal types combined, and what is their overall result? On a long-term chronological basis, can one observe either a slow process of alteration or a breakpoint in the partial system of regulation? The interested reader can consult works such as Boyer (1978) and Mazier, Baslé, and Vidal (1984); the latter summarizes a voluminous quantity of statistical work. The same approach can be used with respect to the mechanisms governing competition (Boyer and Mistral 1978), the money supply (Gelpi 1982), and public spending (André and Delorme 1983a). It has also been applied to systems of international economic relations (Capian 1973; Destanne de Bernis 1977; Mistral 1981; Aglietta 1986). This brings us to the third step in the analysis.

3. From the Conjunction of Partial Logics to the Overall System of Regulation

In reality, nothing ensures that a system of institutionalized compromises, whose regulatory virtues are often only local and partial, will necessarily lead to adjustments permitting the reproduction of the *whole* of the economic system: a sustainable allocation of workers and capital among the various sectors, the compatibility over time of income distribution, credit, demand, etc. However, in this respect, a purely qualitative analysis will not do. This is because it does not allow us to verify whether a set of economic mechanisms all work together coherently or whether, on the contrary, they collectively produce an unfavorable pattern of development or a succession of vicious circles.

It is thus necessary to use *macroeconomic*—and, if possible, *econometric*—modeling of the different partial systems of regulation. The initial aim is to verify the consistency of our logical constructs, and to locate possible weak points in the reasoning. The model thus serves as a criterion for judging theoretical work, not just as a source of empirical support. Next, it also offers a way to propose certain alternatives to existing macroeconomic theories. All too often, there are more preoccupied with deducing the largest possible number of results from a set of axioms chosen a priori than with organizing conceptual research around the major problems of the day. However, it is methodologically unsound simply to oppose the "facts" to theories. How can the former be constructed independently of the latter? Indeed, in a sense, this rejection of any kind of theorization and formalization lies behind the failure of almost every attempt at pure empiricism. According to a harsh but just saying, merely describing "the world is as it is" does not constitute an acceptable counterargument to the neoclassical paradigm. Hasn't this criticism been applied to the American institutionalist school?

Consequently, the regulation school, without hesitation but also without excess, has made use of models. Though often simple enough, they nonetheless have illuminated essential points: the origins of inflation and its persistence in the initial phase of the crisis (Boyer and Mistral 1978); the coexistence of virtuous circles between competitiveness and growth and of vicious circles working the other way around (Aglietta, Orléan, and Oudiz 1980; CEPII 1983, 1984); the sharp changes in the effects of technical progress on employment since the 1970s (Boyer and Petit 1981); or the consequences of new forms of the wage relation (Boyer 1986a) and production organization (Boyer and Coriat 1986). Some radical American economists have for their part developed an analogous methodology, even if their basic concepts and detailed formalizations are somewhat different (Bowles, Weisskopf and Gordon 1983; Shaikh 1978, 1979; and many others).

But it is also possible to examine long-run economic dynamics, which brings us to the fourth component of an analysis.

4. Modeling Regimes of Accumulation in Order to Characterize the Different "Structural" Crises

Purely from a methodological viewpoint, it is important to establish an alternative to the traditional Marxist conception that views accumulation as possessing laws regarding tendencies, which must ultimately win out over transitory and contingent factors. To a history of capitalism that stresses the contradictions deriving from the decline of the rate of profit, regulation theory opposes a more modest conception, centered on understanding the rise and subsequent crisis of regimes of accumulation (Coriat 1982 and Boyer 1979), leaving the question of long-term trends open. It will undoubtedly be necessary to accumulate many more long-term national studies before we can establish general hypotheses running across historical eras and applicable to all known modes of development.

From this perspective, it is necessary to determine the inherent tendencies of each regime of accumulation, which history has shown may lead to the physical elimination of the labor force, to permanent overproduction, or to still other difficulties in the valorization of capital. Schematic formalizations are therefore necessary to see whether deductive reasoning confirms the intuitions drawn from historical analysis. This type of analysis, often underestimated in research inspired by Marxism, has already led to useful conclusions. These have included the impossibility of autoaccumulation in sector I (Aglietta 1974), the reinterpretation of classical models of growth and business cycles (Boyer), and the establishment of a link between the modernization of sector II and the tendency toward a slowdown in France's growth (Bertrand 1983). Last but not least, Fagerberg (1984) has presented contrasting models of competitive, Taylorist, and Fordist regimes of accumulation, each of which is subject to structural crises with specific and distinct origins.

This conclusion is reinforced when one is concerned with analyzing social formations in which the logic of industrial production is not dominant. It then becomes essential to formalize hypotheses about the consequences of a very specific set of productive structures and social relations in a simple macroeconomic model. Thus, representing the dynamics of a country that is principally a primary products exporter, such as Chile (Ominami 1980), or a petroleum producer, such as Venezuela (Hausmann and Marquez 1986), supposes a new kind of macroeconomics which, far from mechanically applying the major theoretical models, sticks close to the realities of the country under study. On this point, the regulation school has come to conclusions similar to those of certain development economists, such as Taylor. It is only in this way that we can explain a phenomenon that represents a paradox for the standard models of underdeveloped economies: why oil-exporting countries can go into crisis when oil prices rise, along with oil importers—though for totally different reasons.

This mention of the development of the current crisis in various countries suggests that my general presentation of the regulation approach leads to two further issues. First, readers of published works on regulation have raised questions about the *consistency* of the approach, pointing, for instance, to the *lack of a single model*. Second, is it not appropriate to judge a tree by its fruits, and a theory by its *relevance*, or, in other words, in terms of the usefulness of its interpretations and its implications for economic policy? Some splendid-looking trees produce nothing at all, while others that seem less impressive provide abundant harvests. In which category should the regulation approach be placed?

3. The Regulation Approach: Assets and Liabilities

It is time to return to chapter 1's critical analysis of regulation theory, and to the balance sheet I began drawing up there. In an era in which economists are seeking a new paradigm capable of responding to the challenges of the 1980s, the details of its theoretical foundations and methodology are ultimately less important than its possibilities for fruitful application. At this point, the reader is probably wondering, "What does the regulation school have to contribute to an understanding of today's problems?" Economists, as well as social scientists in other disciplines, may legitimately be asking, "Is the approach worth investing time and resources in?" As for the members of the regulation school themselves, their accumulated experience leads them to a third question: "In which areas and along which lines should research now proceed?"

This chapter and the next deal with these questions. To begin with, since it is a sound idea to judge the tree by its fruits, I ask what theoretical or practical conclusions the regulation school has reached—about economic policy, for example (section i, below). Next, the consistency and relevance of the paradigm must be discussed, in the light of the numerous claims about and criticisms of the regulation approach in recent years (section ii, below). Finally, since it has both assets and liabilities, and since the general context, along with the intellectual climate, has changed considerably since the 1970s, we must ask which lines of inquiry would allow for the revitalization and reunification of a school that faces a real risk of disintegration. Such will be the object of the next chapter.

i. THE FIRST FRUITS

A look at the regulation approach in perspective—which the distance provided by a decade of work now allows—reveals some broad

67

convergences and points of agreement among most of its adherents, even if all have developed their own viewpoints on details. One would therefore be justified in calling this intellectual tendency a school if it possessed a degree of institutionalization, along with procedures for the critical evaluation of work, which led toward a research program that would develop on a cumulative basis. Five of its major conclusions will be presented here.

1. In the Long Run, Institutions Matter

It was perfectly conceivable that as the number of case studies grew, significant institutional differences might have been revealed, but the overall systems of regulation might ultimately have been quite similar from one country to another. After all, the hypothesis that theoreticians like to postulate is that differences in technology or social structure are of secondary importance compared to a general model.

Yet to the contrary, research by members of the regulation school has revealed *varying* forms of regulation, different both over time and in space. In the case of France, for example, they learned that institutional forms sometimes favor the continuation of the prevailing logic of accumulation, and sometimes undergo a change of orientation and develop along new lines. After several decades, the mode of development itself is fashioned by this new context. Thus, over more than two centuries, three types of regimes of accumulation have come to succeed each other, with the great crises (1848, 1873–1895, 1929, 1967–1973) and the world wars marking the key dates in this process of evolution. However, it seems that the long-run growth rate is highly dependent upon the mode of development. It is moderate when extensive accumulation predominates, weak and erratic in pure intensive accumulation, and strong and relatively stable in intensive accumulation centered upon mass consumption.

However, two points should be noted here. First, the details of *periodization* are a matter for debate even within the school. For example, for Lorenzi, Pastré, and Toledano (1980) the crisis of 1929 was of the same kind as those of the nineteenth century. Likewise, Bertrand (1983) emphasizes mechanisms different from those initially suggested by Boyer (1975). But these can be considered normal, healthy differences because they constitute part of the work of verification carried out within a particular research agenda. (Is it necessary to recall that a similar controversy has raged among monetarists concerning the exact origins of the crisis of the 1930s?) Second, the frequently voiced criticism that the smallest institutional change would change the system of regulation, so that the regulation school would be reduced to saying that everything is always changing, is not really justified. In point of fact, it has isolated only *three* changes in the mode of development over two centuries, with the present crisis marking the debut of a fourth. Moreover, the concept of "structural forms" as used in the regulation approach should not be confused with that of "institutions" as used by the institutionalists. The former are global in nature, and have effects felt throughout the whole economic system. The latter may be quite local in character, with consequences principally at the microeconomic or intermediate levels.

A second noteworthy result concerns the differences between nations. Comparisons of the economic evolution of European countries since 1973 (Boyer 1986a), or of the other OECD countries (CEPII 1983, 1984, 1986; Barou and Keizer 1984) reveal considerable variations within the Fordist model of the virtuous circle of growth. It even seems that the crisis has made more apparent the peculiarities of individual countries, which the strong wave of growth preceding it tended to obscure. In short, many of the differences in national performance regarding growth and employment have been linked to specific characteristics of the wage relation. In this respect, the views of the regulation school are similar to those of the Anglo-Saxon corporatist school, as well as those of certain researchers operating within a Keynesian-institutionalist perspective. On the other hand, their differences with orthodox Marxism and its three stages of competition are substantial, despite terminological similarities, which have led to unfortunate confusion.

2. Every Society Has Fluctuations and Crises Corresponding to Its Structure

Economists usually don't worry too much about the long-term dynamics of the economy, contenting themselves with analyzing series of short-term fluctuations. Even in this case, however, the regulation approach offers a viewpoint that may be of some use. It holds that economic fluctuations—inflation, in particular—depend upon the reigning mode of regulation in each historical era. For example, differences in institutional contexts would explain why recession and deflation went together during the nineteenth century while, on the contrary, rising unemployment and inflation coexisted long after World War II. I am not talking about minor differences within a single general model, but of *different* models that the analyst has an interest in distinguishing.

With these differences taken into account one can understand why the same international disturbance (an oil price increase, rising interest rates, etc.) has different consequences in France and Germany, the United States and Japan, or among oil producers and oil importers. Once this is recognized, it would be vain to insist at all costs on applying a single, ultrasimplified model, whether monetarist, Keynesian, or even Kaleckian, to every case. Everything depends on the precise type of regulation that prevails. This is well known by macroeconomists and econometricians who construct models and run simulations—and all too often ignored by theoreticians. In this regard, it is noteworthy that some macroeconomists feel that they have to explain divergences in macroeconomic performance by particular characteristics of the wage relation or the greater or lesser degree of consensus in existence (Gordon 1984; Davies 1983; Schor 1985). The teachings of the regulation school thus appear far from unreasonable, even judged by the standard of contemporary work in comparative international economics.

In this little game of analogies and distinctions, it is necessary to underline both an *intellectual affinity* and an *important contrast* between the regulation approach and work in economic and social history. In a sense, the title of this section is no more than a variation on Labrousse's famous saying. That is no accident, because my whole enterprise has notable similarities to that of the founders of the *Annales* school (Burguière 1986): the accent on structure, collective phenomena, and forms of organization; the rejection of a dogmatic Marxism; an intent to elaborate a method and a set of questions, rather than a theory; the use of a generative and comparative method; and a willingness to draw on other social sciences. In one sense, this parallel has brought the regulation school close to some contemporary economic historians, particularly those inspired by Marxism (Bouvier, Marseille, Rougerie, etc.). However, the process that the *Annales* school started in 1929 led historians of the 1960s and 1970s to explore new objects of research (the history of mentalities, mores, the family, and beliefs), and to turn away somewhat from Labrousse's aims.

On the one hand, the New Economic History has had its adepts among French economic historians. Their work, using developments in neoclassical theory and econometric methods, has certainly introduced rigor and novel ideas into the field. However, in it the initial hypothesis of *Les Annales* has been almost inverted: social forms are conceived of as *consequences* of the logic of the economy—not the other way around. From this stems the paradox that the 1980s have seen a near-reversal of the traditional positions of theoreticians and historians. The members of the regulation school want to get back to the social foundations of economic activity and appeal for more research in social history. Yet the historians, for their part, have borrowed the assumption of an invariance in time and space from economic theory, and make wide use of econometric techniques (including the most sophisticated, such as spectral analysis) to study economic cycles and crises.

On the other hand, the downturn in growth rates since the 1970s has reawakened interest in the *theory of long waves* proposed by Kondratiev in the 1920s. Since then, the search for evidence of such cycles has absorbed much of the energies of economic historians in the hope of showing that we are indeed today in a descending phase of stagnation, in conformity with the patterns observed over more than two centuries. To the members of the regulation school, the theory's success is rather surprising. First, the empirical evidence in its favor is far from convincing. The trends in prices and volumes are confused, the long-run time series are not really comparable, a breakpoint should have been expected after 1945, etc. Second, no satisfactory theoretical model has been suggested to explain the supposed patterns. References to the limits of the accumulation process usually remain implicit, without leading to the sort of analysis one would expect if one took seriously the concepts of regimes of accumulation or of transsecular demographic models. Finally, while the shift from expansion to crisis is largely endogenous, renewed growth appears strongly dependent upon the political, social, and technological context (which the sharp variability in the duration of the descending phases of Kondratiev cycles would tend to confirm). Why are so many brilliant researchers and renowned specialists fascinated by an approach that in the last analysis is so impoverished, cut off from social history, and far from the ambitions of *Les Annales?* We can only regret that questions about long-term cycles have not led more often to the discovery of the regulation approach.

3. A Novel Theory of Inflation

A continuing series of works by members of the regulation school over the past decade has aimed at developing a theory of inflation that is monetary but not monetarist (Aglietta 1976; CEPREMAP-CORDES 1977; Benassy, Boyer, and Gelpi 1979; Aglietta and Orlean 1982; Lipietz 1979, 1983). Making use of what researchers like Cartelier and de Brunhoff have learned, they have tried to find different combinations of the basic functions of money in the act of exchange itself. In a system dominated by money in commodity form, transactions are tightly limited by the availability of metallic means of payment, so that booms represent a temporary explosion of credit in relation to the money stock. The associated inflation is eliminated in the subsequent phase of recession through the effects of strict monetary constraint. Thus, from the phase of competitive regulation on, the relations between credit and money are at the heart of the dynamics of accumulation, as well as of changes in the general price level. But this is not the only mode of integration of the real and monetary variables.

As the credit system develops, both qualitatively and quantitatively, the causal relations between money and credit are altered. In a pure legal tender system of money credit prevalidates a set of transactions. It is then possible to imagine a new shape for the business cycle. When there is overproduction, expansion of the demand for credit can be a means of postponing the downward adjustment of production or increasing effective demand. Furthermore, the creation of money as public debt increases allows for the pseudovalidation of excess production. Consequently, this new form of money creation is an integral part of the process that generalizes the mechanisms of stagflation. Declining sales with continuing inflation, albeit at a moderate pace, constitutes an essential characteristic of monopolistic regulation.

Inflationary phenomena then reach the heart of the accumulation process. General increases in nominal prices become the means by which the economic circuit is closed, while creating a permanently increasing public debt, which grows in proportion to the difficulties encountered by the accumulation of productive capital. At this point, the works of the regulation school converge with those of the post-Keynesians on debt economies mentioned in chapter 1. This analytical schema is essential in order to explain the reversal of monetary policy that occurred at the beginning of the 1980s. The "monetarist shock" would then be only the expression of a durable shift in relations between debtors and creditors. Soaring interest rates forced the reestablishment of equilibrium in financial structures that accelerating inflation was putting dangerously out of balance. Subsequently, after several years of very high real interest rates, many of the sources of the earlier inflation were eradicated. However, the counterpart to all of this was a blockage of the growth of productive investment, and therefore a tendency to stagnation.

The monetary crisis is aggravated still further if the effects of rising real interest rates on the stability of the international monetary system are taken into account. We owe the development of novel tools for analyzing the growth, maturity, and crises of international monetary regimes to Michel Aglietta (1986) and the economists of the Center for International Forecasting and Information (CEPII 1983, 1984, 1986). We now also possess the elements of a monetary but nonmonetarist theory of international financial relations. Moreover, this analysis has important consequences for economic policy. Is it possible to imagine an international financial system that would be able to work without the dominant economy's money serving as the key currency? If so, in what circumstances would it be possible to establish a new type of currency and a novel set of regulatory mechanisms (Aglietta 1986)? In this regard, the regulation approach resembles that of political scientists like Keohane (1982), who have long studied the same international monetary regimes. Optimists might see this convergence as a basis for an original paradigm applicable in various social science disciplines.

4. Fordism: The Heart of Postwar Growth—and Crisis

There is undoubtedly no use spending much time on this point, which has become the Bible, the trademark, indeed, the token of membership in the regulation school. Basically, transformations of the wage relation have appeared to be one of the chief determinants of long-term changes in the mode of development. This conclusion is all the more significant because the authors involved initially focused, instead, on forms of competition or state intervention, undoubtedly under the influence of the traditional Marxist periodization. From this perspective, the "thirty glorious years" are interpreted as the first example of the more or less synchronized, simultaneous evolution of the norms of production and consumption, which avoided making overaccumulation the principal danger and recurrent depression the sole means of adjustment. Quite logically, the crisis that began in the mid-1960s in the United States (and in 1973 in the other OECD countries), was the consequence of the maturation of Fordism and the rise of new contradictions. The growth of demand was supported by various institutional forms, but structural problems of profitability appeared. Minor differences aside, all the members of the regulation school share this analysis of the situation. It has implications, both for theory and for the future.

Regarding the former, research on the wage relation has once more put the capital-labor relation in the foreground of Marxist analysis, treating it as the key to economic and social dynamics. In the past, researchers in effect focused on competition among capitals (small firms versus large ones) or on the antagonistic or complementary relations existing between public and private property (the market versus the state). Yet that amounted to neglecting what retrospectively appears as one of the most essential qualitative changes in industrial capitalism over the past century. In fact, as Braudel's work suggests, commercial and financial capital has long been internationalized, while lifelong wage labor is a much more recent phenomenon. This innovation bore within it new kinds of social conflicts and economic dynamics. In this regard, the regulation school has explored a series of problems under the rubric of the "wage relation" which unorthodox neoclassicism has analyzed as "implicit contracts" or "efficient salaries." Its investigations thus follow the same lines as those of the major contemporary school which seeks to link economic performance to specific characteristics of the wage relation.

Consequently, the regulation approach has acquired a certain relevance for attempts to clarify the unfolding of the current crisis. As early as 1977, it enabled researchers to formulate the hypothesis that the changes that had occurred after the first oil price increase were structural in character, while most economists' gazes were still fixed on the simple financial and energy-supply disequilibria linked to OPEC's action. Of course, there were other Marxist approaches that had reached similar conclusions—but perhaps for the wrong reasons! The members of the regulation school, for their part, have insisted always that the existing system has reached the limits of its economic, technical, and social conditions of production. By the mid-1980s, the search for alternatives to Taylorism had become so general that this contention had undoubtedly become fairly widely accepted. Such was not the case between 1979 and 1981, when it was first formulated and propounded.

Likewise, *flexibility* as an issue in the strategies of firms and governments appeared early on as one of the key themes in the various sorts of transformations that the Fordist wage relation is undergoing. Thus, it was no coincidence that a work bringing together various investigators' conclusions on this highly topical question appeared in 1986. The comparative research that laid the groundwork had begun four years earlier. Of course, merely dealing with a question at the center of social and political debate does not ensure that it receives correct and entirely satisfactory treatment. Still, isn't it better to seek one's keys near where one thinks they were lost, rather than under dazzling street lamps far from where real economies are to be found? This point leads to a fifth and last teaching of the regulation approach.

5. Economic Policies Must Be Related to the Mode of Regulation in Force—or in Emergence

These considerations converge to suggest a way of *posing*, if not *resolving*, current questions about economic policy. In particular, they suggest that the objectives, instruments, and effectiveness of state intervention are directly conditioned by the configuration of the institutional forms that make up the mode of development. For instance, in a competitive system of regulation, the state limits itself to maintaining the legal and social conditions that make labor power a free commodity and ensure the permanence of the money relation. On the other hand, the development of wage labor and the worker struggles to which it gives rise, along with the progressive detachment of credit from physical money, lead to new forms of state intervention. Providing for the collective aspects of the long-term reproduction of the work force and controlling credit in order to ensure the continuity of accumulation then become two of its essential tasks. In reality, this is less a question of purely ideological choices between laissez-faire and *dirigisme* than of solutions invented under the pressure of necessity with the aim of bringing social conflict and the accidents of the accumulation process under control.

But the crisis of the mode of development precipitates that of most of the relations between the state and the economy. For example, the slowdown of growth after 1973 reduced the tax base, while the preceding institutionalized compromises and the strict application of existing social insurance benefit rules implied the accelerating growth of state intervention. From this, in time, resulted public sector deficits and endebtment, which called most components of state expenditure into question. The fact that such developments were common to countries and times in which governments were of different political persuasions shows the structural character of the crisis of economic policy. Such is the regulation school's explanation for its rapid obsolescence during the past decade, as noted in chapter 1.

At the risk of exaggerating a bit, one could describe the Keynesian versus monetarist dilemma as a choice between a one-eyed person and a fully blind one. The former have perceived, at least implicitly, the consequences of intensive accumulation based upon mass consumption for the management of the public sector. But they seem to have thought that such a regime of accumulation contained no contradictions and was therefore sure to endure. They thus forgot that Fordism—the hidden foundation of Keynes' theory—would not last forever. So much for the one-eyed people! As for the blind, they are none other than the neoclassical conservatives. For them, Fordism is no more than an error of history, a sort of dead end before the good old mechanisms of competitive regulation come to prevail once again. This vision, fashionable today, really amounts to shutting both eyes to economic reality. First, it fails to see the continuously contradictory nature of growth in the nineteenth century, which was hardly as harmonious and virtuous as neoclassical theory and conservative political discourse claim. Second, it is blind to the beneficial changes, both for workers and capitalists, that occurred after World War II. Finally, it ignores what is really at stake in this decade and the next. Are we not seeing a *change and reorganization* of the state's role in the economy, rather than its diminution? Isn't workers' interest in their work a better gauge of competitiveness than the ease with which they can be laid off? Many other examples could be cited.

There is thus some use in seeking to discover the *structural* foundations underlying the successes—and failures—of different conceptions of economic policy. The results are not only a critique, but also a *constructive* contribution to policy formulation, even if some observers have been disappointed by the policy proposals made by members of the regulation school. Part of the misunderstanding stems from the fact that economic policy is conducted on a *day-to-day* basis in response to unfavorable developments. What should be done with the exchange rate? Should taxes be raised or lowered? Should households or firms be taxed or exempted? It must be recognized that the regulation approach provides few direct responses to these questions, no doubt because it lacks what has become the standard instrument for dealing with them: a complete, rigorously estimated macroeconomic model. On the other hand, it does emphasize that the severity of short-term constraints must not hide the more ambitious objective of economic policy in periods of structural crisis: promoting the emergence of a new mode of development.

But it should be emphasized that this approach also leads to another dilemma, that of nearsightedness versus farsightedness. At times, the degrees of openness and indeterminacy in the process of recomposition induced by the crisis are underlined. This is the case, for example, when one opposes defensive flexibility to flexibility that is much more offensive, intensive liberalization of foreign trade to well-tempered protectionism, or the reduction of state intervention to its redeployment. The myopia stems from the fact that the tree can actually hide the forest, because a *minimum* of determinism probably prevails. After all, the scientific method is built precisely on this hypothesis, which has up to now proven far more fruitful than that of order by accident, as Thom (1980) underlined in his critique of Prigogin's model. Alternatively, the regulation approach can lead to the opposite error, a mechanical succession of modes of development. The expectation then becomes the reorganization of the wage relation in a way that resolves the crisis of productivity. Such expectations make this criterion function as a categorical imperative—the source of the farsightedness mentioned above.

Various examples of such errors can be found. One was the warnings of a cumulative depression due to the effects of the liberal policies implemented at the end of the 1970s, which overestimated their real impact. Another was the premature announcement that, because microprocessors had just been invented and the world had swung around to center on the Pacific axis, the crisis was over—in 1976! Such lapses can legitimately give rise to questions regarding the validity of approaches in terms of regulation.

II. DOOMED HERESY OR PROMISING THEORY?

Now that the contributions made by research on regulation over the past decade have been presented, it is necessary to analyze its limitations. Numerous authors have voiced judgments critical of the regulation school, expressing astonishment at the interest attracted by an approach with so many shortcomings. Their critiques have centered on five major propositions.

1. A Description, Not a Theory

The criticisms of so-called "pure" theorists tend to focus on the attention that the regulation approach pays to the social framework of economic phenomena, within its more descriptive and sociological approach to the discipline, as Mingat, Salmon, and Wolfelsperger put it (1985:459). If general equilibrium theory is the model of "scientific" economics, there is no doubt that regulation theory does not lie in the same plane, because it is open to a much larger conception of social and economic phenomena. Does this lead it into the sin of the American institutionalists (the *Journal of Economic Issues*, in particular): merely describing "the world as it is," instead of proposing a representation that is abstract and idealized but causal in character? On reading many popularizers' works, especially those discussing the postwar Fordist era of growth, one would be tempted to agree with this charge. In these works, it is indeed sometimes difficult to distinguish between hypothesis and consequence, affirmation and demonstration, simple description and theorization.

But if one examines the articles in academic journals and research work on which these popularizations are based, one reaches a very different judgment. All that is necessary to arrive at a much more nuanced appreciation is a look at Aglietta's thesis (1974), the CEPREMAP-CORDES report (1977), or the articles that have appeared in *Economie et statistique*, *Revue économique*, *Recherches economiques de Louvain*, or the *Cambridge Economic Journal*. In these works the theoretical framework is explicit, and explanatory hypotheses are tested against institutional history and quantitative time series. As a result, the conclusions—whether true, false, or uncertain—are by no means tautological. It cannot be said that they consist of pure and simple description based upon "the immediate experience of non-initiates and their everyday knowledge," or, in short, "on the common sense which has led to the success of a Galbraith," as Mingat, Salmon, and Wolfesperger claim (1985:474).

One need only turn back to chapter 2 of the present work to see that the concepts of institutional forms, regimes of accumulation, modes of regulation, and the typology of crises hardly fall into the domain of description or vulgar economics. They represent a highly theoretical construct, which is not limited to the observation that we live in a world of multinationals, collective bargaining agreements, or increasing state intervention. Such phenomena are related to the concepts of exchange and production relations, themselves derived from the manner in which modes of production are constituted (as reformulated by the structuralist school). As a result, the regulation approach is not a simple journalistic description, but an *attempt at theorization*. Its relevance may be debatable, but not its existence.

It is, however, true that the approach is not situated at the same level of generality as the standard Keynesian or Walrasian model. It posits the possibility of the existence of *various* macroeconomic models, not just one, since the exact form they take is open, depending upon the structural particularities of the society under consideration. Strictly speaking, it furnishes an underdetermined model, which must be filled in with a set of intermediate hypotheses. When the latter are incompletely (or not at all) specified, the professional economist can legitimately argue that description is replacing analysis. This gap is particularly evident for social formations that do not belong to the center, which is composed of dominant, long-industrialized capitalist economies. To this day, the typology of regimes of accumulation remains largely a hypothesis to be verified by more empirical studies. (See, in this connection, the suggestions made in chapter 4.) On the other hand, the criticism holds far less well if one is interested in the post-1945 economic dynamics of the major OECD countries. The hypothesis of Fordist growth has received a *precise* formulation in terms of the traditional categories of macroeconomic analysis, as the various models available attest (Boyer and Mistral 1978; Bertrand 1983; Fagerberg 1984; Boyer and Coriat 1986).

Consequently, it is surprising that some writers who are ultimately fairly close to the regulation school, criticize it as lost "in a sort of wonder before the diversity of the world, beyond the richness of descriptions" (Galibert and Pisani-Ferry 1986:27). Their criticism seems aimed at some *further* developments of the methodology originally tested on the United States. Within the logic of Fordism, certain specific national characteristics—the wage relation, for example—have been found to explain notable differences in macroeconomic performance. Is it mere description to underline that Great Britain is characterized by restricted Fordism, West Germany by flexi-Fordism, and Italy and Spain by tardy Fordism (Boyer 1986a)? Or, on the contrary, is this not a fuller, more precise observation, analogous to those resulting from the English-speakers' theory of corporatism? One would hope that an examination of recent work by adherents of the regulation approach would lead the reader to the latter conclusion.

There is, on the other hand, a much better founded criticism. A. Noël (1986) argues that the members of the regulation school frequently refer to the role of institutions in the origins of individual and collective behavior, but do not ask enough about their raison d'être. In other words, the approach lacks a *real theory* of institutional forms. Chapter 2 sketched out some preliminary thoughts in this regard, without, of course, offering a complete, general theory of their functioning. The present definition owes far too much to a legalistic Hauriou-type definition (p. 32), and not enough to contemporary work on the question. Noël therefore justly calls for a rapprochement with what he terms neoclassical institutionalism and its application to questions such as those regarding international regimes. But one can also extend such research to the question of the wage relation and its treatment in unorthodox contemporary neoclassical approaches. It is thus no surprise that among the new research perspectives proposed in chapter 4, the question of theories of institutions occupies a prominent place.

Description can indeed mask a refusal to theorize. However, the adherents of the regulation approach, for their part, have never thought that a good description could replace a pertinent theoretical abstraction.

2. A New Misadventure of Institutionalism?

Mingat, Salmon, and Wolfesperger (1985) have, in effect, taken the theory of regulation as an example of contemporary heterodoxy. The heart of their argument is that in many respects it is just a new wrapper for an old approach: the institutionalist-historicist school. They ground their argument on a series of closely argued criteria that distinguish "heterodox" theories. While they often hit sensitive spots, they nonetheless considerably underrate the distinctiveness of the regulation approach. To show this, a more detailed review of their criteria and arguments is in order.

There is little doubt that the regulation school dissents from the dominant theories in the discipline. A rejection of the concept of general equilibrium is common cause among all its members, representing a decisive step in their personal intellectual itineraries. But it is less clear that they all aim to construct an alternative theoretical framework as axiomatic and rigorous as general equilibrium theory. Such a goal is sometimes expressed by Aglietta and Orléan, but other writers have set themselves a different task: understanding the overall dynamics of macroeconomic systems without going all the way back to their most abstract foundations—individual rationality, the theory of value, etc. Moreover, the questions that regulation theory seeks to answer are much narrower than those of neoclassical theory, whose ambition is to cover all of economic activity and even social life (witness the imperialism of rational choice theory in economic sociology: the theory of the family, criminality, education, social inequality, etc.). Those who would make regulation theory into a global alternative to the prevailing orthodoxy are heading straight toward a severe disappointment.

Such disappointment is frankly expressed by Galibert and Pisani-Ferry (1986). But their expectations are ill-founded, because the questions, methods, and aims of the two approaches are different. Moreover, one represents part of a dominant, long-lived tradition with universalist ambitions, while the other is still in its infancy, supported by a tiny minority within the profession, and obviously limited in its orientation. Comparing the extremely dense intellectual network woven by the neoclassical tendency with the output of a small circle of authors is like comparing a knit sweater to a fish net. (Furthermore, the members of the latter group themselves display an irrepressible zest for differences!)

Besides, the *second* of our critics' criteria underlines the difference in object between the approaches. They note that institutionalism, like the regulation school, is interested in long-term *structural transformations*, not in the functioning of a given economic system or that of one of its parts. It is in this sense that one can speak of "evolutionism." For the most part, this characterization is entirely correct, all the more so if one refers to Destanne de Bernis' and Aglietta's initial works. Experience showed, however, that the discovery of the laws governing the transformations of the system remained beyond the economist's reach, and that the quest for such laws represented a concession to the determinism of historical materialism.

Thus, influenced by both the problems of the day and the need to communicate with scholars of other theoretical persuasions, the researchers using the regulation approach have concentrated on formulating partial theories concerning a particular mode of development. They describe the historical succession of various regimes of accumulation and modes of regulation, not why such a succession was necessary. Today, however, the relative uncertainty regarding the conditions required for the resolution of structural crises has become an obstacle to understanding what is at stake in the crisis in the 1980s. Understandably, then, the research program presented below poses the question of the long-run evolution of economies in new terms. It asks: How have the capitalist economies resolved previous great crises? How can we today recognize the restructuring of the mode of development, or the emergence of a new one?

According to the *third* criticism, the gestalt-holism so dear to the members of the regulation school leads them to fall into a typically *functionalist* conception of society. It is true that the definition of regulation, by stressing coherence and compatibility, may justify this criticism. Such critiques were formulated by the end of the 1970s. For example, de Brunhoff (1980) saw a striking antagonism between the functional nature of regulation and the dysfunctionality of structural crises. Yet although it refers to a real tension, this criticism is not entirely accurate.

First, current work within the regulation approach emphasizes the *permanent duality* between the forces making for cohesion and the tendencies towards breakdown among the different institutional forms. Its Marxist origins, and the accent it places on the transitory unity of contradictory factors (on which Alain Lipietz's comments in Appendix I are quite illuminating) prevent it from falling into a mechanical functionalism. Secondly, it is not correct to say that great crises are purely functional. On the contrary, they mark the *limits* inherent to a given order. Nothing guarantees that they will lead automatically to a new configuration of the system. In this regard, economic analyses of the period from 1965 to 1985 are worth rereading: the chaotic, uncertain nature of the transformations underway and the alteration of periods of euphoria and pessimism are quite evident. Regulation theory is thus not a sort of functionalism. At best, one can note the reestablishment of the coherence of previously contradictory elements after the fact. The most that can be said, then, is that it is a sort of semifunctionalism observable afterwards, not before the fact.

Another alleged weakness of the regulation approach is its supposed technological reductionism, only slightly tempered by the accent placed on cultural factors. It should be noted at the outset that the argument is somewhat contradictory, because the defining characteristic of institutionalism is precisely the integration of technological change into the framework of a much broader analysis of society. More specifically, the emphasis on Fordism does not represent a sort of "determination in the last instance" by technology. On the contrary, production and consumption norms result from very specific wage relations and forms of competition, not from the mere application of mechanization and automated production techniques (Coriat 1978). Likewise, the current quest for flexibility is not simply the consequence of the microelectronic revolution in production. Rather, it involves a groping toward and testing of alternative forms for the internal organization of firms and wage relations (Boyer 1986a).

The final criticism concerns the supposed excessive interest of the regulation school in "the big problems, involving the major concerns of our society." In a word, it is said to suffer from *globalism*, which is all the more regrettable for the fact that its members are "capable of macroeconomic analysis in conformity with the norms of the profession when they are dealing with smaller issues" (Mingat, Salmon, and Wolfesperger 1985:466). That economists should interest themselves in the major questions of the day is hardly blameworthy. One might even regret that the great theoreticians do not descend into the arena of social debate more often. Besides, since the regulation theorists have made these structural transformations the subject of their research, they have every right to apply the results of their work to the political controversies of the moment. Unfortunately, the most urgent social problems cannot always be represented by simple and elegant models—so it is sometimes necessary to forego the charms of method and formalization. Of course, the stands then taken have a sizable subjective component, even if they are based on analytical work that generally holds up quite well when judged by the usual criteria of scientific worth. But is such the case only for this school?

It is therefore quite unfair to see the regulation school as solely motivated by *political* commitment and incapable of analyzing the slightest issue because based only on moral indignation on behalf of

83

the "categories of people whom the socio-economic system renders the most unhappy and least free" (Kölm 1986:276,266). It is true that its members' intellectual work is much more closely related to a declared commitment to the left than is the case for many other scholars. Can all their analyses be called "ideological" and "political" because of this? One has only to glance again at the results summarized in the preceding pages to put this claim into perspective. The *convergence* between results produced via the regulation approach and those of researchers using very different approaches merits attention. Finally, in an era in which methodological individualism has triumphed, perhaps it is not so bad that a group of economists seeks to demonstrate the operationalizable character of a completely different methodology, even if only to present new questions to orthodox researchers. These include: what is the role of institutions? How can structural unemployment be explained? etc.

Ultimately, this determination to uncover new problems and concepts, to forge tools for analysis and verification, is a break with the institutionalist tradition in the strict sense. Mingat and his colleagues recognize this themselves when they note that "the regulation approach can escape the sterility of the 'pure' inductivism (to the extent that such is possible) of the 'historicist' variant of institutionalism, in which monographs accumulate without producing any new general knowledge" (1985:472). The regulation school is thus an institutionalism that has borrowed a great deal from Marx, Kalecki, Keynes, structuralism, and the *Annales* school, not a mere repetition of an approach whose recurrent failure has been shown by the history of economic thought.

Moreover, it resembles an analogous trend toward the *renovation* of traditional institutionalism resulting from work on labor economics (Piore 1979), technological change (Sabel 1982), or development economics (Taylor 1983). The common characteristic of both approaches is that they start from a structural and historical viewpoint and arrive at a combination of institutional analysis, formalizations, and quantitative results. The difference is considerable when compared to the dichotomy evident in the work of a Mitchell (1930), who makes references to Veblen on the one hand but presents a purely empirical analysis of the workings of business cycles on the other. Yet the regulation approach has not escaped a still more serious criticism.

3. The Absence of an Analytic Method

The criticism common to all the writers who have approached the regulation school starting from the canons of standard theory is that it lacks a proper method of analysis. This convergence of views suggests a real problem, which has three elements.

In one sense, the "absence of an analytic method" refers to the globalism of the regulation approach, which makes the part (a given institutional form) depend on the whole (the mode of development). In this way, the *social relation* receives primacy over the *individual*, so that one can legitimately ask what the latter's place is in the analysis. This premise means that in regulation theory one never finds an abstract *homo economicus* who represents the basis for the study of the logic of the adjustment of production to social demand. The overall properties of the system are not a simple geometric projection of the behavior of a particular part or individual. This is only another way of expressing the regulation school's commitment to a holistic approach, joining a structuralist but "historicized" Marxism with a Keynesian macroeconomics founded on the paradoxes of the passage from the micro to the macro level.

For all that, there is no harm in asking, "How is it possible that individuals, in doing their best to further their interests within the possibilities open to them, are unable to question the prevailing institutional forms?" At this point in the discussion, it is undoubtedly appropriate to refer to the attempts that have been made to reinterpret Marxism in the light of the tools of neoclassical theory. (I am referring chiefly here to Roemer's work, and secondarily to Morishima's.) For example, Roemer has shown how an endogenous division of different individuals into the classes of capitalists, wage earners, and independent workers can occur. He has also redefined the concept of exploitation via an approach in terms of game theory. One might thus imagine an *overall framework* that defines the essential rules of the game, then an *individualistic approach* explaining how various individuals find their places within the existing relations of production.

There is nothing to prevent the construction of the macrosocial and institutional foundations of a microeconomic theory along similar lines. Haven't anthropological studies revealed the extraordinary relativity of the concept of rationality? It would be abusive to reduce it only to that of *homo economicus*. Likewise, studies of organizational behavior have indicated the extremely limited nature of the domain of real optimization, and the importance of empirical procedures or conventions leading to results that are merely satisfactory rather than optimal in the sense of neoclassical theory. It may turn out that the theory of economic calculation plays more of a normative than an explicative role in the analysis of effective behavior. In short, in emphasizing routines, conventions, and legal procedures, the regulation approach may not be as far as it might seem from a treatment of economic decision making in capitalism as it really happens (and not in the idealized capitalism necessary for the magnificent theorems of Walras' theory).

This criticism also has a more precise theme, focusing on the inconsistency in the passage from the individual level to the collective level in the case of Fordism. Thus, Kölm voices doubt that " 'capital' increases the workers' purchasing power, initially through wages, so that they can buy its products" (1986:274). The point is completely justified, and underscores again the danger of a success based upon fashion, obtained through the popularization of an extremely simplified version of a process that the members of the regulation school know to be much more complex. In fact, the criticism bears more on the *vulgarization* of their work than on the central concepts of the analysis. First, it is utterly erroneous to make capital into a homogeneous, unified entity conscious of its own interests. Competition is the rule, cooperation the exception, so that entrepreneurs actually try to reduce the wages of their own workers, even as they entertain the contrary desire for a rise in the level of economic activity to increase their demand and competitiveness. If, on the contrary, they raise wages, they will worsen their competitive position, while their gains in terms of extra demand will be tiny, even in the case of an enormous conglomerate. The contradiction between the individual and collective interests of capitalists is therefore patent.

Thus, explaining the transition to Fordism requires us to bring in several different, interrelated factors. To start with, workers in every firm were engaged in a general struggle for salary increases. During the 1950s, the practice of industrywide contracts, or the diffusion of wage norms from a few key enterprises to the whole of the economy, ensured parity in wage increases across almost the whole of the economic system. Subsequently, wage increases supplied the basis for expectations of the general growth of demand. Insofar as firms established their prices on the basis of a margin added to production costs, the competitive position of each was not affected. This eventually led to the establishment of a Fordist regime of accumulation, perhaps *facilitated* by Keynesian policies of demand stabilization. Once again, the passage from the micro to the macro level is not a simple projection. (In this respect, the appellation "Fordist" is undoubtedly poorly chosen, since it evokes the conscious strategy of one individual, rather than an overall social process.)

In fact, studies of the auto industry by experts have shown that the innovations introduced by Ford were responses to difficulties in managing labor (increasing absenteeism, productivity problems, etc.), instead of being directly linked to a macroeconomic objective. Moreover, the Ford assembly line in the classical sense went into crisis in the 1930s. The result was that the Model T was replaced by annual model changes, in line with the strategy General Motors had elaborated in response to slackening demand (Hounshell 1984). On this point, earlier work of the regulation school reflected a somewhat cavalier position. We would thus benefit from a greater familiarity with the work of historians of firms and production techniques, with whom a permanent dialogue would be desirable.

An example one might cite would be the research now underway into the new contracts negotiated in the Renault factories during the 1930s. At first they clashed with the prevailing form of regulation. Once the rules governing the *whole* of the industry had been changed, the contracts operated so as to favor the emergence of a new system of regulation. The detailed results of additional studies of individual enterprises conducted within the framework of the regulation approach undoubtedly could help give it the analytical precision that overly general presentations have lacked. Beyond that, they would offer a response to the critics who point to the focus on manufacturing industry in the Fordist model and its underestimation of work in the tertiary sector (Delaunay 1985), as well as to those who contest the proposed overall periodization, particularly the dating of the transition to intensive accumulation (Barrère, Kebadjian, and Weinstein 1984).

Finally, a third methodological criticism concerns not the logic of our construction, but its *nonfalsifiability*, in Karl Popper's sense. Thus, Mingat, Salmon, and Wolfesperger (1985:472–473) stress the difference between an interpretation and a test: "Once they have managed to *interpret* the facts, the members of the Regulation School feel no need to test anew . . . analyses which seem to them sufficiently validated by the efforts they made to give a unique and coherent *meaning* to disparate bits of data." For example, they regret "the remarkable lack of effort to verify a central element in the reasoning of the regulation theorists, which is the phenomenon of the diffusion of wage increases from sectors termed 'motor sectors' to the rest of the economy" (Mingat, Salmon, and Wolfesperger 1985:474). According to them, the statistical data presented are merely illustrative, and the regulation school's sole means of convincing outsiders would be shared sympathies.

On the specific question of *wage determination*, the point is particularly ill-taken, because the necessary statistical and econometric work has indeed been done to demonstrate the existence of this essential trait of monopolistic regulation. First of all, the hypothesis of the uniform diffusion of wage increases has been tested, and shown to be specific to the contemporary period (Boyer 1978:36, 47 for the nineteenth and twentieth centuries, respectively). Subsequently the role of the capital goods industry as a "motor" was shown to be considerable (Boyer and Mistral 1983a:39–42). Finally, it is utterly abusive to speak of mere illustrations: the cursory nature of the argument in Benassy, Boyer, and Gelpi (1979) should not obscure the number and variety of statistical tests performed, an idea of which can be gathered from the voluminous research report produced (CEPREMAP-CORDES 1977). Moreover, the object of these tests was a specific hypothesis: do changes in the institutional features of the wage relation imply equivalent changes in the elasticities of salaries with respect to prices, industrial production, unemployment, and so on? That is hardly a simple tautology.

As proof, one can note that the econometric research on this question has shown, for instance, that there is a delay of approximately twenty years between institutional changes and their repercussions for the determination of actual wages. It is thus an optical illusion to imagine that the results of statistical tests were only presented to support previously elaborated conclusions. The same demonstration can be made regarding forms of competition. The rise of monopolistic structures is certainly observable after World War I, but previous mechanisms for the determination of profit margins persisted. In other words, the regulation school does not content itself with grand, Toynbeean historical panoramas. Its work has—or can have—a definite analytical and empirical content.

Indeed, one of its contributions has been the introduction of the regular use of *econometric* techniques into Marxist economics, which has traditionally been extremely reluctant to use formal models and statistical methods. This said, it is unfortunate that the proportion of hypothesis-testing work has not been greater, and that the works most frequently cited (and criticized) are indeed analyses that a hostile observer could perhaps put on the dusty shelves of the philosophy of history. There are two possible solutions for this. First, one might hope that it is possible to reverse the corollary of Gresham's law which seems to hold that citations of minor articles or general overviews drive out those of essential works. To give an example, the members of the regulation school were only too pleased that some of their works were published in the journal *Problèmes économiques*, which is well known for its wide circulation and impact. On the other hand, they could only regret that it was their simplest —indeed, most simplistic—pieces that were brought to the awareness of the knowledgeable public, while other, more important ones remained in obscurity! But it would also be appropriate for them to alter their style and orientation of their research, so that the testing phase of every study of regulation is conducted with particular care. This is an *irreplaceable* aspect of the approach (see chapter 2), and it has many potential applications, as can be seen from the number and variety of possible lines of research (see chapter 4).

4. The Growth and Crisis of Fordism: Where's the Model?

Both Noël (1986:34) and Kölm (1986:273–275) have noted the absence of rigorous tests of the regulation school's hypotheses regarding the origins of the current crisis. At first glance this criticism may seem paradoxical, since its members diagnosed the beginnings of a structural crisis quite early—in the mid-1970s. Since then the crisis has come to occupy such a prominent place in social and intellectual life that its very obviousness has tended to eclipse the search for an analytical clarification of its *origins*. It must, in fact, be recognized that the explanations offered are both too numerous and insufficiently connected. To run through them briefly, they include the saturation of consumption norms, the rise of the tertiary sector and unproductive labor, the crisis of productivity within Fordism, the disconnection between national economic spaces and accumulation on an international scale, and the loss of hegemony by American capitalism. Depending upon the case, emphasis is placed on the influence of social conflict (strikes by semiskilled workers, demands hostile to the system), on technological factors (the counterproductive character of large production units, their rigidity vis-à-vis short-term fluctuations), or the contradictions inherent in the long-run tendencies of the regime of accumulation (inflation, a distribution of income unfavorable to profit, etc.).

Thus, the tasks of clarification, hierarchization, and synthesis appear to be particularly necessary today, if only to clarify what is really at stake in the crisis. According to whether the limits are social, technical, institutional, or economic, the corresponding solutions would obviously be quite different. Besides, researchers using the regulation approach are well equipped to undertake such a project. First of all, the growing number of comparative international studies allows them to identify more precisely the relative importance of the factors that determined economic performance, both before 1967 (or 1973) and since. Is it not significant that the countries that tinkered with the Taylorist principles of work organization (Japan and West Germany) have done the best in an unfavorable international conjuncture? Second, and above all, it is difficult to evade the salutary discipline of formulating and testing an econometric model representing the essentials of Fordist logic (see chapter 4, sections I and II).

It should thus be possible to specify to what extent, the crisis is due to the domestic productivity crisis and to what extent, on the contrary, to the breakdown of the international financial system, the differing policy implications of these two alternatives being obvious. If the first is preponderant, the essential task is to negotiate a new wage compromise in which workers would have a direct interest in improving productivity and quality of output. If, on the contrary, the second is dominant, then ways to coordinate economic policies, or better still, the rules and disciplinary mechanisms of a new international monetary system, must be sought. Or will it be necessary to combine both of these strategies in the appropriate proportions?

Research along these lines should provide an answer to two sorts of objections to the work of the regulation school. The first holds that the characteristic properties of the different modes of regulation have not been adequately identified (Galibert and Pisani-Ferry 1986:27). The second argues that rejecting the notion of equilibrium would render difficult both dialogue with neoclassical theory and any form of modeling (Mingat, Salmon, and Wolfesperger 1985:463). The question of equilibrium merits a specific response, because the term is too often assimilated to the meaning given it by general equilibrium theory. In that sense, it is the property of a system in which price and quantity adjust themselves simultaneously, so that supply and demand are always equal. In contrast to this conception, the regulation approach stresses the dynamic processes that make unemployment, bankruptcies, inventory accumulation, and excess productive capacity permanent features of capitalist systems. It would then be necessary to speak of disequilibrium, as does the theory that goes under that name. But this would take as a permanent and unavoidable point of reference Walras' concept of equilibrium, which is quite specific and hardly operative in real economies which have no general auctioneer to equate supply and demand. Thus, it is necessary to adopt a broader definition: "Any *status quo* situation of the system, in which there is no reason why an endogenous force of change would come into play, corresponds to an equilibrium" (De-Vroey 1984:5).

On that basis, one could build a model that includes the various mechanisms considered to be important, and define the solution of the system as "equilibrium," taking into account its past history, differing adjustment rates, and a certain number of variables considered exogenous. I can therefore only agree with Mingat, Salmon, and Wolfesperger when they note that "what distinguishes neoclassical 'orthodoxy' from the Regulation School's 'heresy' . . . is less the usefulness of reasoning in terms of equilibrium than the manner of doing so" (1985:464). The question is which *variables* are considered pertinent, the *mechanisms* on which they depend, and even more, the division between the *endogenous* and the *exogenous*. For example, in order to translate the simultaneous determination of production and consumption norms into mathematical terms, it is necessary to have a model in which technical progress is largely endogenous and real wages are sensitive to differences in the configuration of the wage relation. More generally, the dynamics of every economy are related to precise configurations of institutional forms, so that they may be destabilized by long-term changes affecting one or another. Such an approach has been used to analyze the consequences of greater flexibility in nominal wages (Boyer 1986a) and productive organization (Boyer and Coriat 1986).

Once the major variables have been incorporated and the notion of equilibrium has been redefined, modeling various modes of development would be a good way to reinvigorate work on regulation. First, the concept of *structural crisis* will be reevaluated and specified. It is defined by the following property: when the system leaves its zone of structural stability as a consequence of the endogenous or exogenous evolution of the model's parameters, one observes a simultaneous reduction in the growth rate, a fall in the rate of profit, and the appearance of economic fluctuations of great amplitude. All of these are characteristics of a great crisis. Second, initial tests bearing on the United States have produced a periodization that is not exactly the same as that of previous work. In short, the regulation school has much to gain from this effort at analytic rigor. A concern for formalization would have the additional merit of addressing a fifth and final gap.

5. A Political Commitment, But No Program

Certain critics, including some far from the regulation school and others close to it, have emphasized a supposed paradox. They maintain that, although committed to the left, economists of the school are ultimately unable to define a policy program measuring up to the expectations and challenges produced by the present crisis (Mingat, Salmon, and Wolfesperger 1985:485; Galibert and Pisani-Ferry 1986:28). Ironically, one could reply that economists of the French Communist Party or self-proclaimed Trotskyites have delivered just the opposite verdict. Their theoretical journals regularly condemn the members of the regulation school for having inspired the policies followed by the Mitterrand government after May 1981! These policies are regarded as the application of the school's reformist program which, moreover, is considered totally inadequate to meet the needs of the time. It must be said that members of the regulation school were the first to be surprised by such charges of paternity. In general, they have had the opposite impression, namely that their ideas have had little impact—rarely regarding analysis, almost never in the formulation of policy proposals. But political and ideological debates often have their own rationale, which has little to do with reason itself. So I will keep the discussion on a strictly analytical plane.

For some, the origin of the regulation school's difficulties in this respect lies in an erroneous conception, or at least in an underestimation, of the *role of the state* in contemporary capitalist economies. This recurrent critique has been voiced by Keynesians (Kölm 1986:286) and by Marxists using the state monopoly capital approach (Barrère, Kebabdjian, and Weinstein 1984), as well as by the Grenoble wing of the regulation school (GRREC 1983; Destanne de Bernis 1983a).

According to the Keynesian tradition many, indeed almost all, of the roots of the crisis reside in inappropriate economic policies—specifically, unduly restrictive monetary policy both in the United States and the international economic system (the "monetarist shock" of the 1980s, the spread of the deflationary policies preached by the International Monetary Fund, etc.). Training in macroeconomics and attentive readings of Keynes by most of the members of the regulation school lead them to think that the question is not so simple. As was previously stressed, economic policy is not autonomous with respect to the prevailing mode of development. Policy is its complement and auxiliary, not necessarily its pivot. One of the contributions of regulation theory has been to distinguish clearly the *motor* of the postwar growth (Fordism) from the *brake* and the *accelerator* (namely, countercyclical stabilization policies, alternately expansionary and restrictive). In the last analysis, the breakdown of the Keynesian orthodoxy in economic policy is not simply due to the swing toward conservatism. It is just as much *endogenous:* the acceleration of inflation, the steadily decreasing impact of reflationary policies on employment, and the loss of coherence in national productive systems.

The *Marxist* critique is focused on another level, that of the *theory of the state*. In reality, the regulation school has adopted a view that corresponds much more to the theories of Poulantzas than to those of Lenin and contemporary Marxist orthodoxy. No, in its view the state is not just the concentrated expression of the power of monopolies, because it constitutes the totality of a much wider set of compromises—of industrial capitalism with the peasant world, of a modernist fraction of capital with the majority of the work force, etc. This explains why, during the crisis, subsidies to firms grow more slowly than transfer payments, which would be denied by the simplistic conception of state monopoly capital theory (though not by its more sophisticated variants). In the last analysis, the state is permanently subject to two contradictory imperatives: on the one hand, supporting accumulation; on the other, legitimizing existing social relations. Moreover, French history is rich in episodes in which the latter has taken precedence over the former (the end of the nineteenth century, the 1930s, etc.). More fundamentally, the growth of state intervention is not necessarily an indication of a silent transition to socialism. Far from being antagonistic to the logic of the market, in many cases intervention acts as a support for it. It should be underlined that the regulation approach leads us to deemphasize the cardinal opposition between *private* and *public* property.

Instead, it focuses our attention on the wage relation as a relation of production and submission, faithful to a tradition originating in the work of Bettelheim. (At this point I should call attention to the possibilities that the regulation approach opens for understanding the societies of Eastern Europe. One should think, for example, of Andreff's concept of arhythmic Taylorism (URGENSE 1982), and of that of regulation through shortage proposed by Chavrance (1984).

There is, however, no doubt that this embryonic theory of the state needs a lot of development, given that research has thus far concentrated on its *forms*, and not on its general *foundations*. Can one therefore claim that, by remaining at a high level of generality, the members of the regulation school have revealed their inability to define any pragmatic political program whatsoever, as do Mingat, Salmon, and Wolfesperger (1985:475)? The argument is supported by two out-of-contest quotations from Aglietta and Orléan's *La violence de la monnaie* which are held to prove that "they have nothing to say about anything whatsoever." In fact, the content of the work cited gives just the opposite impression. These critics also stress the extreme *diversity* of the policy recommendations coming from within the regulation school, and their limited applicability. It is true that the rapidly growing corpus of articles and books published by members of the school has sometimes produced contradictory positions on various specific points (such as openness toward the international economy, the appropriate exchange rate, etc.). It has also happened that particular writers have changed their views on economic policy as their research has advanced, and that observed changes lead to new questions. However, these divergences, although significant, should not hide the essential point: the existence of a large measure of agreement on the core of a medium- to long-run economic policy program that is intended to promote the emergence of a post-Fordist model of development.

The school's first contribution, a very general one, is its refusal to treat the choice of the best policy as a matter of dogma applicable at all times and in all places, as if it were based on a single universally applicable model. One can thus perfectly logically propose a devaluation of the franc and a revaluation of the Deutschmark, once one has analyzed the effects of these measures on two very different industrial structures (Aglietta, Orléan, and Oudiz 1980). Similarly, a policy which proved astonishingly effective for resolving the crisis of the 1930s may be totally inadequate in the new mode of development now being constituted (Boyer and Mistral 1983b). Thus, reflation through public spending and wage increases could be helpful in the 1960s—including May 1968—yet no longer stimulate employment in the 1970s, when the international context was one of stagnation and industrial structures had become fragile. In debates usually conceived in terms of general theories and dogmas, the regulation approach may paradoxically appear eminently pragmatic and relativistic. In some ways it recalls the unorthodox structuralist tendency in development theory, which insists on the specificity of national characteristics rather than the global monetarism and free trade propounded by the international financial organizations (Taylor 1986).

The second major contribution of the regulation school concerns the various components or premises of a medium- or long-term economic program adapted to the specific characteristics of the 1980s. It has been suggested that overvaluation of the national currency should be avoided, since it can uselessly aggravate deindustrialization. It has also been pointed out that technological changes now underway might eventually revive the productivity growth rate, but may aggravate the problem of unemployment within previous forms of organization. Consequently, an industrial modernization policy is no substitute for an active employment policy. In this respect, one should not confuse the most regressive forms of flexibility (an unimpeded right to lay workers off, part-time forms of employment, the establishment of a lower minimum wage for young people) with a recomposition of the wage relation that combines social progress with economic efficiency (integrating tasks of execution and control, improving general and technical education, giving workers an interest in the firm's results, a high wage policy).

In fact, the regulation school's proposals touch on policies in numerous fields. These include: the construction of poles of competitiveness on the basis of intensified exchanges of information among firms, the state, and intermediate organizations; the medium-term stabilization of agreements between large firms and subcontractors; the creation of jobs at the crossroads between the public and private sectors meeting needs unsatisfied until now (the environment, assistance to elderly people, new types of child care, etc.); the need to reform the financing of national insurance, shifting the burden of some payments (family allowances) from wages alone to the totality of incomes; and the transformation of the ecu[1] into an international reserve currency, in order to combat the omnipotence of the dollar

1. Translator's note: The ecu, or European Unit of Account, is a proto-currency created by the European Economic Community.

and better face up to the possible breakup and fragmentation of the international monetary order. Can one really accuse the regulation school of having nothing to offer in terms of economic policy proposals?

Does, however, this set of policies represent a *coherent strategy* for overcoming the current crisis? In the present state of affairs, lacking the analytic precision that can be attained through a proper econometric model the adherents of regulation theory cannot compete on an equal footing with those whose job consists of making day-to-day studies of the impact of different economic policy measures. This explains the disappointment experienced by some public sector decision makers and economists who are responsible for economic studies and predictions in the bureaucracy (Galibert and Pisani-Ferry 1986:28). But one can legitimately ask whether the role of the regulation school is to compete with the various research teams that interest themselves in these questions today. Is its role not rather to draw attention to the *long-run stakes*—the structural changes or possible perverse consequences of a series of short-term decisions? In short, the regulation approach falls within the tradition that made up one of the essential functions of French planning: illuminating long term perspectives.

As to changes through *social compacts,* that is something that cannot simply be decreed! In this respect, it is regrettable that the proposals of the regulation school have not been the object of wider debate, and that none of the existing social actors or political tendencies have seized upon them. Had they been subject to a flow of demands and critiques, its members would surely have been encouraged to develop programs that are more clearly thought out and more relevant than those they have so far produced. It may be that the decline of liberal euphoria will come to make this question a topical one in the next few years, but this is a hope, and far from certain!

In conclusion, beyond the simple repetition of a vulgarized version of Fordism, the yield of results has been far from negligible. That is a good criterion for measuring the relevance of a theoretical approach. After all, after interminable detours of deductive logic, how many theories lead to trivial propositions that are ill-founded, if not totally unrealistic, in the light of the actual characteristics of contemporary economies? By choosing the opposite tack, and emphasizing theories directly linked to some major problems, the regulation school has sought to contribute to the understanding, and even the explanation, of the "thirty glorious years" and the glum decade that succeeded them.

But the critics have justly underlined the multiple shifts, approximations, and major inadequacies that mark the approach. Even if one may disagree about the consequences to draw from them, the problems and challenges posed are real and considerable. At the end of this rapid overview, one is tempted to conclude with the remark of one of our Canadian colleagues: "There is something not quite right with the theory of regulation. So much the better—let's get to work!" Henceforth, the regulation school can no longer excuse its problems as the growing pains of infancy. It must face up to its crisis of adolescence with an innovative frontal attack on some of the most formidable—and, until now, neglected—questions.

4. Toward a Second Generation of Work: An Agenda for Research

The preceding discussion has indicated the current limitations of the regulation approach. Once these have been recognized, further work within the paradigm cannot simply repeat past research on a larger scale. Essentially, the conceptual framework must become more precise and refined, new questions must be asked, and, even more important, new, more rigorous analytical methods must be elaborated in order to reduce some of the uncertainties that still plague regulation theory.

To meet the requirements of sound epistemology, the task will involve defining both the hard core of the theory and its outer protective shell. One would be tempted to include at least three fundamental hypotheses in the first category:

■ The accumulation process plays a determining role in the overall dynamics of the economy.

■ The economy is not spontaneously self-equilibrating through the workings of the market and competition alone.

■ Institutions and structural forms play a determining role in guiding this process via a set of individual and collective behaviors.

As to the outer shell, it must be neither too small (because the theory is then reduced to its core, and cannot be extended to other domains), nor too large (in that case no empirical observation can invalidate the construction). In the case of the neoclassical theory of individual choice, we know that the variability of the system of constraints and the breadth of what is considered to be external to the economy constitute this protective shell. For the regulation school, we could say that it is the differentiation of institutional forms as they have been forged by the history of the various national spaces.

98

But it is then necessary to come up with testable models that can be provisionally accepted or rejected in light of the available information.

However, the proof of the pudding is in the eating: the epistemological validity of a theory is shown by *putting it to work*. It would therefore be utterly pointless to try to resolve in the abstract what must be shown by day-to-day usefulness in a field of research. So I will instead propose six major lines of research that a second generation of works utilizing the regulation approach might follow.

I. MORE CASE STUDIES TO ENRICH THE THEORY

Until now there have been two ways to do research on regulation. The easier one has been that of the *copycat*, pious and faithful, which I had occasion to mock back in chapter 1. The more "exotic" the economic formation studied and the less experienced the researcher, the weirder the results. It is, however, worrisome that some members of the regulation school have displayed similar inclinations, thinking that they could characterize social formations quite different from those of the center on the basis of results obtained concerning the advanced capitalist economies. They have had trouble resisting the temptation to define North-South relations and the situation of some semi-industrialized countries in terms of the Fordist mode of development. In this respect, the concept of *peripheral Fordism* certainly has its attractions. It has thus enjoyed a certain degree of success among young researchers from the Third World, winning a larger audience for the regulation approach. Yet one might wonder whether this victory has not been a Pyrrhic one. It involves the confusion of the technical bases of Fordism (the assembly line, etc.) with its economic and social characteristics. In the latter sense, Fordism is essentially the linkage of the norms of production and consumption over a given economic space. Once this is understood, it is a contradiction in terms to apply it to a case in which the international division of labor and the international division of consumption are markedly out of synch.

As to the empirical relevance of such a theory, it is easy to see how it can lead to problems. To call Brazil, for instance, an example of peripheral Fordism amounts to ignoring a number of the country's characteristics: the small size and influence of the industrial work force and its limited access to mass consumption; the divergence

99

between real wages and productivity, even in the modern sectors; the fluidity of the wage structure; the diversity of production and consumption structures; the role of the middle classes in durable goods consumption; major problems in the articulation of agriculture and industry, etc. Besides, isn't it ironic that the authors who chose this approach after attacking dependency theory have forged a variant that is just as mechanistic? They underestimate the country's internal social dynamics, turning it into the simple projection of a regime of accumulation on an international scale. In short, the whole methodology of the regulation approach is turned upside down!

What is needed is an entirely different research strategy: using the *method*, not its *results* to analyze and define other modes of regulation and development. I will not expand here on Hausmann's exemplary work on the Venezuelan economy (1981), which shows how industry represents only a secondary element resulting from the dynamics of the state's oil rent. It would be fruitful to consider the objective to be the fulfillment of the research program begun by Ominami (1986), and produce a rigorous, relatively complete typology of regulation systems. This would suppose that a *specialist* who knew the history of each country well would follow the various steps used to analyze the economic development of the United States and France (described in chapter 2, section v).

This question concerns not only the South, but also some of the advanced countries. Thus, Cassiers' study of Belgium (1986) analyzed the regulation of an economy that is largely open to international trade. Her work is far from the Fordist-Keynesian model and close to a reformulation of the model of the competitive economy. This leads her to an original interpretation of the crisis of the 1930s, which is far from a carbon copy of the crisis of Fordism. Likewise, Aboites (1986) has shown that the relationship between agriculture and industry explains the peculiarities of a noticeably non-Fordist pattern of industrial development in Mexico. His results seem to be confirmed by an initial overview of the Brazilian case by Velasco e Cruz (1985). The history of these countries could become the subject of original studies, which might produce interesting results that would help us understand their current difficulties (Soria 1985).

In this manner, the intermediate concepts and specific models could gradually be elaborated, making the regulation approach into a genuine alternative, both for the analysis of the problems of developing countries and as a theory of the growth of the older industrial capitalist economies.

II. MODELLING MODES OF REGULATION IN THE DOMINANT ECONOMIES

The initial attempts to analyze the regulation of the dominant economies today need critical reevaluation. Is it possible to formulate the core of a model that combines as best we can what has been learned from a decade of formalizations without an attempt at a synthesis? The ideal would be to bring together in the same model two essential traits of the approach:

■ the *wage relation*, in both aspects: as a system of production organization and of remuneration; *and* as a major determinant of productivity, the wage-profit division, and the level of employment, as well as

■ the interrelations between *credit* and *money*, and their roles both in exchange flows and in the financial structures of accumulation.

The simpler the formulation the better, in order to focus discussion on what makes the regulation approach different from the others. The establishment of a basic model, which would be an equivalent of what the IS-LM scheme represented, would undoubtedly clarify a lot of arguments that still suffer from a certain lack of precision. Furthermore, the traditional macroeconomic variables (exchange rates, interest rates, fiscal policy, etc.) must be introduced, so that it will be possible to resolve one of the frustrations evoked above, namely: just what does the regulation school propose in terms of short-run economic policy?

It should be underlined that this is not an isolated effort, but rather one that corresponds to similar projects underway in other countries. For instance, there are specialists in the study of technological change (Nelson and Winter 1982) who are seeking an *evolutionary* model that would permit the simultaneous analysis of changes in technology and institutional forms (Dosi, Orsenigo, and Silverberg 1986). Likewise, Marglin (1984), has tried to set out the broad lines of an "unorthodox standard" macroeconomic model, even if the name is a little perplexing. Nor should it be forgotten that some radical American economists have been working in this field for several years, and their results suggest that some interesting syntheses are on the way.

Like nature, it seems, specialists in macroeconomics abhor a vacuum! More specifically, they cannot oppose the new classical models simply by objecting to the lack of realism in their initial hypotheses. The point is not really comparing "reality" to a model, but rather confronting different models against each other to see what they teach us about real economies. It is for this purpose, not in the name of a somewhat dated ideology of "pure science," that modeling is a useful technique in social science research, though not to the exclusion of other methods.

Essentially, what has been suggested is the elaboration of a purely theoretical model. However, it could later prove useful to develop a *macroeconomic* model on that basis, which could be tested against the evolution of the economies of the United States, France, and other OECD countries over the postwar era. The first attempts to do so—those of Bertrand (1983) for France and of Bowles, Gordon, and Weisskopf (1983) for the United States—have already produced some interesting, if not definitive, propositions. Such work could lead to a third area of research, at the crossroads of economic history and modeling.

III. THE ORIGINS OF GREAT CRISES

In truth, until now, the members of the regulation school have juxtaposed their theoretical approach to descriptions of the sequence of events leading to the current crisis more often than they have actually tried to combine them. Consequently, on the one hand we have a general approach, and sometimes the outlines of a model, and on the other a description of the different factors that may explain the slowdown and instability of growth. Various writers have criticized this dichotomy, underlining that the interpretations thus presented, although perhaps plausible, have not received a real demonstration.

Concerning the analysis of the current crisis the criticisms are much more specific. How could slow changes in productivity and profit rates explain the sharp fluctuations that occurred from 1974 to 1985 (Kölm 1986:273)? The question merits particular attention in light of the results of Bertrand's simulations (1983), which suggest that the increasingly heavy technical composition of capital should have led to a gradual slowdown of growth rates, without the wide swings that have actually marked the course of the crisis in France. It must be recognized that a reconciliation of the structural factors making for crisis with the specific ways in which it develops remains to be worked out. Toward this end, two research strategies can be envisaged.

The first would consist of a search for a pattern of changes in the characteristic structural parameters of the system of regulation that would tend to destabilize the regime of accumulation and mode of regulation. Starting from the results produced by a theoretical model —the object of the preceding section—one could verify whether the mid-1960s actually do represent a swing from a zone of structural stability to one marked by deteriorating profit rates and short-term instability. It would also be interesting to simulate the consequences for accumulation and growth of the crises in the organization of labor, although it might prove impossible or excessively difficult to do so. For example, one might introduce exogenously an increasingly heavy capital coefficient, a deterioration in the relation between productivity and growth, or increases in nominal and/or real wages.

The second method is, in a sense, still more ambitious. It would consist of formulating a long-term model based on adding the dynamics (exogenous or endogenous) of the key parameters governing the mode of regulation to the short-term model. Thus, as Billaudot and Gauron suggest (1985), one might study the consequences of the spread of Fordist production methods. They hold that such techniques, while initially allowing savings of both capital and labor through the replacement of earlier forms of organization, later proved less and less advantageous, as their simple extension gave way to their deepening through the intensified substitution of capital for labor. This method could be used to examine most of the other components of the mode of regulation, such as the endogenous extension of the wage relation and thus of transfer payments, the effects of continuing inflation on decisions about investment and debt, the effects of the internationalization of production and exchange on prices, etc.

Another important point that requires clarification concerns the distinction between the pure Fordist growth model and the form it takes in a *given national economy open to the outside world.* As much as the crisis of the wage relation may explain the internal tendencies toward blockage of the growth process, the instability of international financial and commercial relations has played a preponderant role in the connected sequences of events observed in the medium-sized OECD economies over the past two decades. From this would emerge the possibility of untangling the internal and international factors, thus explaining, for example, the significant reductions in growth in most European countries, particularly in France. This approach would also allow us to distinguish more precisely between three levels of analysis:

- the origins of the crisis in the United States, the country that played a pivotal mode in the postwar mode of growth;

- its transmission to the international financial and money markets and its propagation to the other OECD countries; and

- the interrelations of events from 1973 to 1985, viewed as the result of interaction between the dynamics of the international economy and the national systems of regulation, which are themselves affected by the rise of internal tensions.

This method and program of research could be extended to the earlier great crises, those that began in 1872 and 1929, with England in the place of the United States, to the extent that the necessary statistical data are available.

IV. THE LOGIC OF INSTITUTIONS AND FORMS OF ORGANIZATION

The preceding chapter underlined the role of institutions and organizational forms in capitalist regulation and sketched out some hypotheses about them. However, the precedents of American institutionalism and German historicism warn us against limiting ourselves merely to taking account of institutions. Just stressing their permanence is not enough to challenge the hypothesis that—among economists, at least—generally makes the market and competition into the beginning and end of economic life. It is also necessary to spell out their *specific logic,* which is not simply an epiphenomenon of the logic of commodities or necessarily an obstacle to the spontaneously reequilibrating forces of the market.

In fact, relations between markets and nonmarket forms have always been at the center of social scientific debate, whether one accepts a John Hicks–type vision of the continuous extension of the former, or Karl Polanyi's opposing thesis that the economy, by destroying the social, leads to crisis. Marx himself saw the emergence of large-scale capitalist firms as the consequence of competition and the substitution of the order of the factory for the "anarchy of the market." This led to Hilferding's analyses, and to those of the state monopoly capital school, which make the dynamics of capitalism give rise to its dialectical opposite: socialism and overall planning of economic activity. Closer to the questions that concern us, the debate about whether there should be more or less state intervention underlines the poverty of contemporary economic theories concerning institutions and organizational forms.

This leads to a monumental research agenda: examining the different theories of institutions to find those that best fit with the regulation approach. During the last few years, neoclassical theoreticians have been particularly active in this respect. They have sought to present state intervention, large firms, and the wage relation as responses to market failures (externalities, uncertainties, risk-aversiveness). But one of the debatable points of this approach is that it makes institutions the consequence of the pure logic of the market, contrary to the teachings of history. For example, the state seems to have been born from the power to levy taxes (that is, an appropriation without a direct counterpart), and is thus in violation of the equal exchange involved in commodity relations. Likewise, large-scale firms with various divisions would derive their superiority through the mobilization of returns to scale: job specialization, the role of the dimensions of equipment, and the effects of diversification on vulnerability to uncertainty. There is no doubt that these theories shed interesting light on many contemporary phenomena. However, they have a rather teleological aspect, since they make the criterion of efficiency the selection mechanism for the various organizational forms. In that, they take the same line as the old Marxist orthodoxy, which makes the growth of the productive forces the principal determinant of the transformation of social relations—albeit with some delays and at the price of revolutions!

Consequently, the theoretical work necessary for a detailed understanding of the bases of each system of regulation will have to take another tack. A priori, it would seem that the theory of games, both noncooperative and cooperative, would offer an ideal basis for such a program of inquiry. It focuses on conflict over the appropriation of the results of economic activity, the possibility of coalitions among social groups, and the endogenous origins of sets of rules (when the repetition of a prisoner's dilemma–type game shows how costly noncooperative strategies are). There may also be conflicts over the rules of the game themselves, not just over the results within the framework of a set of conventions accepted by all. Such analyses would certainly be extremely complex if one were considering only purely abstract situations. It would, however, be much easier—and no less enlightening—to apply the tools of game theory to historical episodes in which studies have already pinpointed the relevant institutional forms. These could include:

- Study of the contradictions linked to the emergence of *collective procedures* for wage bargaining. For example, in the 1930s, this involved industrywide agreements as a means of stabilizing competition and of making wage income not just a harmful cost to the *firm*, but also an element of overall demand favorable to the *whole economy*.

- Analysis of the swing away from Fordist wage agreements at the beginning of the 1980s, in an analytical framework that combines game theory and the determination of the level of economic activity by a simple macroeconomic model (first Keynesian in a slightly open economy, then one of an economy in international competition).

- Research on the stability of a given form of competition, taking into account overall expectations, differences in costs and capital intensity among firms, and characteristics of the evolution of the economy at the macro level. For instance, one might look at the process leading from price war to stable oligopoly with mark-up pricing (from the interwar years until the 1950s) and vice versa (since the end of the 1970s.)

Likewise, it would be useful to undertake a critical analysis of theories that examine the differences between the wage relation and pure commodity exchange. Over the past decade, some neoclassical theorists have advanced interesting hypotheses and models concerning the hierarchy of responsibilities in the firm, labor control, the role of information structures in response to technological change and uncertainty, etc. Keynesianism, for its part, has the merit of regarding nominal wages as determined outside the market—unlike ordinary goods—but does not explain their level, which is said to depend on the sociopolitical and institutional context.

As to real wages, *The General Theory* holds their level to equal marginal productivity, which is tantamount to eliminating many of the problems at the heart of economic policy debates in the 1970s involving the indexation of wages and their divergence from productivity trends. Thus, it may be helpful to seek means to define the specificities of the wage relation regarding wages, labor discipline, and work intensity, in the traditional Marxist distinction between labor and labor power (Bowles 1985). More precisely, various forms of labor control can be distinguished according to whether emphasis is put on mechanization, control by foremen, or the incitement offered by the individual's wage under a given social insurance system (Bowles and Boyer 1988).

Another substantial research program could involve the forms of monetary constraint and financial institutions. If previous work has revealed the need for a monetary system that combines centralization and fragmentation (Aglietta and Orléan 1982), it is important to define the principles that lie behind the various configurations observed. The ideal would be to combine a theoretical approach with the results of comparative international studies of the relationship between industrial and financial capital. Then, the secular trends and conjunctural changes in capital accumulation would be determined by motive forces specific to each period: the logic of pure self-financing, the integration of banks' and industries' strategies, or the minimization of the risks of control in a system dominated by financial and stock market logic (Lazonick and Foley 1986).

In this way, one of the frequently noted gaps in previous research on regulation could be filled: the lack of a sufficiently detailed treatment of investment and its determinants. In turn, such a conception of investment as the reflection of an *institutional* structure could not but have an effect on macroeconomic models, while also renewing the old debate on the three determinants of investment: profitability (past or anticipated), expected demand, and the financial constraints of solvency.

The task ahead is already so vast that one hesitates before proposing two additional lines of work.

v. THE ORIGINS, RISE, AND DECLINE OF INSTITUTIONAL FORMS AND THE RESOLUTION OF MAJOR CRISES

The regulation school's concentration on the postwar era of growth led its members to stress the *coherence* of the set of institutional forms stabilizing the prevailing regime of accumulation. Of course, Aglietta's initial work focused upon their long-run transformation, and even sought laws governing the process. Today, it appears an extremely complex one, and far less teleological than supposed by orthodox Marxists—or by regulation theorists at the outset. But in the light of the changes observed over the past decade, the hypotheses of the stability of the Fordist wage relation (Boyer 1986a), forms of credit management (Aglietta 1986), and the forms of state intervention inherited from the postwar era (André and Delorme 1983b) are no longer tenable. The *transformations* of these institutional forms have been so rapid that a whole new series of questions today presents itself. How can the disappearance, circumvention, or questioning of organizational forms be explained? To what factors should the invention and spread (or failure to spread) of institutional forms be attributed? Under what conditions does an embryonic, *marginal* form of organization impose itself on the whole of the system, to the point where it fashions its *overall* logic?

The question poses some difficulties for economists, whose typical research strategy has been to avoid any reference to institutions. It is also true that the process of abstraction which, beginning with Adam Smith, led to modern general equilibrium theories seems to have been more effective than the opposing attempt to begin from institutions and history in order to construct theories. Even the "unorthodox neoclassicists" who take social forms seriously limit their analyses to showing their universal, atemporal logic. The capital-labor relation would thus flow from the concentration of individuals who are more risk-aversive on the side of the workers, and of those who are less so on the side of the entrepreneurs. Similarly, the theory of implicit contracts explains a degree of stability in the wage relation. Yet in neither case do the authors ask whether these forms of organization are *historically contingent.* Consequently, there is a need for research on a long-neglected question, even within the context of methodological individualism: the set of factors on which the emergence and stability of institutions depends.

From the regulation school's perspective, it is tempting to relate these theoretical questions to the teachings of economic and social history, in a permanent process of feedback. This would first involve seeking out the distinguishing factors in the appearance, for example, of a wage relation of indeterminate duration. It may be that the division of labor and the returns to scale associated with it, along with the specific investments linked to internal training within the firm, play a much more determinant role than risk-aversiveness. The wage accords of the postwar era would then correspond to a specific, *historically determined* form of internal firm organization (Williamson 1975, 1985), rather than a general principle, as orthodox neoclassicists suppose (Hess 1983). From this emerges the possibility of explaining the process involved in the genesis and spread of codifications of the wage relation.

We already possess the results of a great deal of historical research and numerous case studies on forms of production organization, the division of labor in large-scale firms, systems of remuneration, and methods of managing the work force and the length of the work day. Further investigation would involve examining the pertinence of the various available theoretical models in specific cases. If satisfactory results are not obtained, it would be appropriate to establish new hypotheses, on the basis of historical experience, to "inject" into the models. The task will undoubtedly be difficult, calling for a certain eclecticism, but it has the potential to offer valuable contributions. This is especially true because the case study is an exemplary technique for applying the regulation approach to problems such as the transition from Taylorism to Fordism, the shift from individual remuneration to essentially collective wage determination, or the emergence of the components of the social wage (workmen's compensation, pensions, family allowances, etc.).

Naturally, the same approach should be applied to all institutional forms, not just the wage relation. The forms of competition, the nature of the monetary constraint, position in the international system, and the structural determinants of state intervention are all equally worthy of attention. Once this is done, however, a more general and difficult problem appears. How does a set of institutional forms become a system, that is, come to define a viable mode of development? The question, in other words, is that of clarifying the process by which great crises are resolved, which until now has remained a mystery to our contemporaries, to economic theory, and to the members of the regulation school themselves! Although discussions of the question have traditionally belonged more to the philosophy of history than to the social sciences in the modern sense, it would be illuminating to confront, against the historical record, several of the interpretations that have been proposed of the resolutions of the Great Depression of the nineteenth century and the crisis of 1929. There are three major sets of interpretations that require analysis.

1. The first stresses the preponderant role of ideas in the establishment of the basis for new forms of regulation. Thus, Keynes would be the theoretician whose work legitimated and illuminated

new practices for the conduct of economic policy, the management of wage negotiations, etc. But it would then be important to show how this new vision of regulation was propagated. One would undoubtedly arrive at the surprising discovery that the New Deal, Popular Front, and Scandinavian Social Democrats ultimately owed fairly little to the Cambridge economist's ideas and a great deal to sociopolitical compromises. At most, Keynes would have furnished the lexicon or grammar of a story written by the social actors. It would also be necessary to make certain that such an interpretation did not fall into a form of *retrospective illusion* by studying, for example, the enormous variety of solutions to the crisis that were proposed at the time. It would be a fascinating task for historians to seek the reasons for the failures—and successes—of ideas about economic reform.

2. One is tempted to replace the preceding hypothesis of *revelation* with that of a *mosaic*. In this second interpretation, conflicts among social groups lead to a set of conventions or institutions governing the different components of the economy's dynamics. But nothing ensures that the latter, the result of local, relatively immediate strategies, will define a viable overall system of regulation. It is certainly the function of economists and specialists in other social sciences to think about the conditions of this process of reproduction. But it is generally beyond their power to impose their conceptions on the myriad of practices involved in market economies and pluralist democracies. From this would arise a concept emphasizing a selection process among forms of organization, oscillating between chance and necessity. It should be underlined that this vision is neither pure functionalism nor a disguised social Darwinism, but combines these two theoretical references in a complex mixture. The role of economists then becomes examining whether it is possible to base a medium- to long-run system of economic and social reproduction on the partial compromises that they observe. *Economic theory would then become the child of history*, and not the opposite, as the New Economics supposed.

3. Finally, according to a third conception, mutually advantageous compromises guaranteeing the cumulative growth of surplus would be born out of the repetition of conflicts that proved ruinous for the parties involved (Schotter 1981; Aoki 1984). Experience of the negative consequences of a strategy of "every man for himself" (within the firm between managers and workers, at the international level between rival countries, etc.) would lead to conventions, insti-

tutions, and legal rules ensuring more satisfactory results (indeed, Pareto-optimal outcomes, to use the language of the theory of individual and collective decision making). In short, *cooperation* would be a *means of resolving conflict,* much as Hobbes argued. The state, and more generally, political institutions, would then take on their full importance, not as the central actors responsible for the conscious regulation of the whole of the society, but as the vectors of the most important compromises at the level of the collectivity. This focus on the *political instance* opens up interesting perspectives. In particular, it might explain why different countries have not found similar solutions to roughly analogous economic problems. Thus, international comparisons between examples of success (the Scandinavian countries) and failure (England) in the search for "dynamic compromises" could prove quite illuminating.

But the long-term historical approach and comparisons with previous structural crises are not enough for economists, who must also face up to the challenges of contemporary problems.

VI. ATTEMPTING TO DISCERN A RESOLUTION OF THE CURRENT CRISIS IN REAL TIME

Concern for the breakdown of the post–World War II mode of development and the groping search for an alternative is common to all the members of the regulation school. On the other hand, their predictions are quite varied regarding the precise elements that might make up a new system of regulation. It must again be stressed how large is the subjective element in each author's analysis of the transformations underway, so it is difficult to avoid the dual dangers of nearsightedness and farsightedness noted above. Consequently, it would be quite helpful to submit the intuitions suggested by the changes over the past decade to rigorous analytical treatment.

As an initial approach, comparison of the present day with the great depression of the late nineteenth century may hold considerable interest. It would seem, in fact, to be more analogous to our own time than does the crisis of the 1930s, the object of previous comparative analyses. Specifically, this would involve detailed comparisons of changes in the wage relation, forms of competition, state intervention, and the international system. The point of departure could be a somewhat simplistic yet stimulating question: has the

United States today entered a phase of decline analogous to that of the United Kingdom at the end of the last century? The study of similarities and differences in the two countries' patterns of macro-economic evolution (productivity, investment, profit rates, etc.) and of institutional and technological innovation could constitute the beginnings of more systematic comparisons.

Given, however, that the mode of regulation is fundamentally different a century later, one could not expect the current crisis to be a simple repetition of previous ones. It is therefore necessary to examine the novelties and the resurgences that have become evident over the past two decades, and not just to accept a Kondratiev-type long-term logic. Consequently, it is important to consider the various innovations that today affect almost all institutional forms in the capitalist economies. Ideally, this could stimulate a wide-ranging *interdisciplinary* project, because economists are hardly the social scientists best placed to analyze social change. At the most, they can examine its consequences and their compatibility in the economic sphere (which, moreover, is difficult to isolate from the others). Under the general rubric of observing social and economic change, I could envision four successive steps.

1. A Typology of Institutional Innovations

Establishing a typology of institutional innovations does not mean producing an exhaustive description (which is in any case beyond reach, since a 1:1 scale map would hardly be useful). Rather, it involves setting out the relations between the various innovations (and, in some instances, regressions) and the key aspects of the crisis of Fordism. Thus, for instance, with respect to the wage relation, the transformations now underway could be connected with various forms of flexibility, which may be understood as an attempt to overcome the inherent limits to the preceding mode of growth (Piore and Sabel 1984; Boyer 1986a; Glyn, Hughes, Lipietz and Singh 1986). This initial work should be enriched and supplemented by more detailed research and extended to other components of the mode of regulation. Toward what forms of internal organization and competition are *firms* evolving? Are we witnessing a significant change in *life-styles* that involves a breakdown or change in patterns of mass consumption? What might be the impact on labor relations and the organization of production? How is the network of *state interven-*

tions being redeployed? Is the present *international system* viable in the long run? What are the consequences of financial deregulation for the links between industry and banking and the relations between money, credit, and accumulation? This simple enunciation should enable one to see the variety of specialties and disciplines necessary for this undertaking. The need for a minimum of coordination of the *initial hyipotheses* in the different domains should also be evident.

2. The Determinants of the Spread of New Forms of Organization

One of our most common assumptions is that all that is new faces a brilliant future; we forget the multiplicity of possible causes of failure of which the history of technology, social welfare law, company organization, and so on offer many examples. Specifically, a first look would suggest that innovations can be both useless and premature when the rules of the game within the firm or the macroeconomic context are not adapted to them. (One could recall the resounding failure of the first Fordist entrepreneurs in the 1930s.) It is therefore essential to examine what determines the spread of the innovations to which the current crisis is giving rise. The comparison of a multitude of cases and/or comparative international studies will, one hopes, give rise to causal hypotheses. In this regard, the *study of failures* is no less illuminating than that of successes. It has the advantage of avoiding many teleological interpretations and of posing the problem of the micro-macro transition—namely, that from individual discoveries to the establishment of new norms.

3. Local and Overall Changes

There is also another danger: getting bogged down in anecdotes and minor changes, when the objective is an interpretation of overall patterns of change. In conformity with a typology forged by the specialists in the study of technical change, it is necessary to differentiate between a *marginal innovation* within an unchanged logic and a *structural change* that affects this logic itself. In addition, the new can be more or less grafted externally onto the old in a third pattern of change, so that it may be a generational replacement (of workers, equipment, etc.) that allows for the transition from one mode of regulation to another. It is therefore important to classify innovations and regressions in relation to this typology on the basis of two criteria. First of all, the *centrality* of the technical or institutional form must be considered: the potential impact of the skateboard is not quite of the same order as that of the microprocessor. Second, its greater or lesser rate of diffusion in the initial phase of the crisis should be noted, since there have been numerous cases of failure after considerable hopes were raised. It is, in fact, appropriate to underline the erratic character of the evolutionary processes that are customary in the great crises. Rare are the variables that shape the future, those whose continuous and rapid growth points to the outlines of the coming mode of growth (in the 1930s, for example, electricity consumption would have been one, but not auto sales.) Thus a fourth and last step is necessary.

4. The Structural Compatibility of the Changes Underway

Together, the various proposed studies may well lead to a question that, though formidable, cannot be evaded. If the observed tendencies continue, are contemporary economies headed toward a *change,* a *circumvention,* or, on the contrary, a *reorganization* of the preceding form of regulation? This question involves neither predictions nor forecasting in the traditional sense of the term. Much more modestly, it is rather a matter of the logical *coherence* and sociopolitical relevance of the final shape of the system if the transformations underway continue. In particular, it is out of the question to try to describe the *route* leading to the new system, since a multiplicity of factors, which are often entirely contingent, help fashion the process. Less ambitiously, researchers can only hope to apply to it some criteria of probability. How, at the microeconomic level, are the recurrent conflicts and disequilibria that manifest themselves being resolved? On the macroeconomic plane, does the conjunction of partial compromises and of new institutions define an overall system of regulation—that is, a set of mechanisms for the attribution of capital, labor, money, and credit that are compatible among themselves?

It is at this level that the macroeconomist can construct purely theoretical models that indicate what the consequences of different organizational forms would be for the growth rate, the dynamics of profits, the level of employment, etc. To put it boldly, one might call such an exercise *macroeconomic fiction.* Although extremely difficult, it is necessary in order to introduce some clarity into the frequently confused political debates regarding the choices confronting society. For the left, for example, it would be important to show that various configurations—not just one—are possible, according to one's value judgments concerning inequality, solidarity, and lifestyles.

This chapter has presented a research agenda that is enormous, difficult, and complex. In short, the reader may judge it to be completely unrealistic—and doubtless it is. However, these sorts of perspectives are necessary to respond to the challenges posed by the regulation approach—and, even more so, to those posed by the scope of the changes that the present crisis is bringing about.

Appendix 1. The Concept of Regulation: Comparing Definitions

MICHEL AGLIETTA

From the preface to *Régulation et crisis du capitalisme* (Paris: Calmann-Lévy, 1976); English edition, *The Theory of Capitalist Regulation: The American Experience* (London: New Left Books, 1979); pp. 13, 16.

> To speak of the regulation of a mode of production is to try to formulate in general laws the ways in which the determinant structure of a society is reproduced. . . . [A] theory of social regulation is a complete alternative to the theory of general equilibrium. . . . The study of capitalist regulation, therefore, cannot be the investigation of abstract economic laws. It is the study of the transformation of social relations as it creates new forms that are both economic and noneconomic, that are organized in structures and themselves reproduce a determinant structure, the mode of production.

From the foreward to the second French edition (Paris: Calmann-Lévy, 1982):

> One should try to avoid using the term "reproduction" either in the sense of a self-perpetuating invariant or in that of an outcome to social contradictions which is *a priori* predictable. All that is reproduced is the problem of socialization: how can social cohesion exist, despite the discord of social conflict? This is the problem which the concept of regulation attempts to confront. Contrary to the currently fashionable interpretation of Marxism, it does so without resorting to any teleological hypotheses. The theory of capitalist regulation is that of the genesis, development, and disappearance of social forms, in short, of the transformations which the separations constituting capitalism undergo.

117

Appendix 1

JEAN-PASCAL BENASSY

From *L'Inflation dans la régulation des économies capitalistes* (Paris: CEPREMAP-CORDES, 1977), vol. 2:

> The regulation of an economic system refers to the set of processes which govern the allocation of factors of production, their utilization, and the division of income.

From "Régulation des économies capitalistes et inflation," *Revue économique* (1979), vol. 30, no. 3:

> By "regulation" we understand the dynamic process of the adaptation of production and social demand, that is, the combination of the economic adjustments associated with a configuration of social relations, institutional forms, and structures.

Reference is made to the definition offered in Gérard Destanne de Bernis, *Relations économiques internationales* (1977), vol. 1.

GERARD DESTANNE DE BERNIS

In his critique of general equilibrium theory, *Revue économique* (November 1975), p. 924:

> Introducing historical time into economic analysis thus does not seem compatible with the central hypothesis which general economic equilibrium (GEE) represents. It seems, in contrast, possible to do so by replacing it with the principal hypothesis of the classical economists (Smith, Ricardo, later Marshall) and Marx, that of the regulation of the capitalist economy by the workings of its own laws of functioning. . . . Such an analysis of regulation would enable us to retain the decisive contribution of Walras's concept of GEE, the affirmation that all the participants in the economy find themselves permanently involved with a set of relations with all the others, but from another perspective, in the framework of another central hypothesis. But the condition of so doing would be taking the economic variables into account by distinguishing their rates of evolution, which implies distinguishing the different levels, and thus distinct sites, of regulation, these different levels, sites, and procedures constantly reacting upon each other.

In this regard, the author refers to Canguilhem's general definition of regulation (see below).

In *Relations économiques internationales* (1977),

> In the long run, the overall system evolves under the influence of the major trends: population growth, the increasing complexity of production techniques, growth in the size of firms, the general structuring of space. . . . Inversely, in the short run, the immediate functioning of the economy is ensured within the framework of the logic of maximizing the rate of profit. This logic expresses itself through two major tendencies . . . [namely, the decline of the rate of profit and the equalization of sectoral rates of profit]. These two sets of tendencies and countertendencies require an adequate set of institutions (and not just state institutions) in order to function. These institutions furnish the intermediate level of regulation of the system, which changes over an intermediate period, the institutional structures having a considerable life, but nevertheless being destined to disappear.

In *Théorie de la régulation et historique des crises* (Paris: GRREC, 1981), pp. 174–175, regulation is defined as

> the process of the articulation of the two laws concerned with rates of profit, inasmuch as they condition the process of enlarged reproduction. . . . Each of these two laws being incarnated in specific forms in each period, . . . their articulation necessarily takes different forms from one period to the next.

ROBERT BOYER

From "La Crise actuelle: Une mise en perspective historique," *Critiques de l'économie politique* (1979), no. 7/8, p. 11:

> We will use the term "regulation" to designate the set of mechanisms involved in the overall reproduction of the system, given the state of the economic structures and social forms. This system of regulation lies at the origin of the short- and medium-term dynamics of the economy. . . . Its long-run dynamics, for their part, do not simply result from the succession of these fluctuations and cycles. A crucial role is also played by political and social struggles which, while partially determined by the dynamics of accumulation, cannot be reduced to it.

Appendix 1

ROBERT BOYER AND JACQUES MISTRAL

From *Accumulation, inflation, crises* (Paris: Presses Universitaires de France, 1978), pp. 3–4:

> Thus, the capitalist mode of production appears to be a structured, dynamic totality. These two aspects have not received the same attention in the Marxist literature. This approach leads to the replacement of the concept of market equilibrium, treated as the universal regulator of individual behavior, with that of reproduction, which condenses all the practices necessary for the deepening of the constitutive social relation of the mode of production, wage labor, treated as a structural invariant. . . . Expressing the logic of capitalism in the language of its structures, this approach describes its dynamics in terms of its reproduction, so that the regulation of the mode of production becomes a necessity. . . . This points to the inadequacy of theoretical constructs involving only the laws regarding tendencies governing the reproduction of the mode of production. Knowing the historical laws of the expansion of capitalism supposes that the variations in the forms of regulation over time and space are constituted as the object of scientific investigation.

From "Crises et régulation de l'économie capitaliste," in Research Group on the Regulation of Capitalist Economies (GRREC), ed., *Crise et régulation* (Grenoble: Presses Universitaires de Grenoble, p. 63:

> We can schematize the functioning of capitalism in the form of a system involving three major sets of variables, distinguished by the way in which they change:
> —*Regular* (which we have already enumerated);
> —*Subject to short-term fluctuation:* essentially, but not exclusively, price and quantity, which change according to specific laws;
> —*Subject to discontinous evolution,* such as forms of competition or of state intervention. These variables could be termed "institutional," with the reservations that this term must be specified by adding that an institution is the product of "a social armistice" (Hauriou), that the settlement of conflicts requires the choice of a procedure which is itself the object of conflict and struggle, and finally that these variables possess a degree of adaptability in response to the overall evolution of the economy and society. . . .
> The social procedures of regulation are by nature part of this third set of variables. Over the whole of the period in which they

120

"correspond" to the state of the variables in regular evolution, they ensure the necessary adjustments among the variables subject to short-term fluctuations. Thus, for the length of the period under consideration, these three sets of variables can be articulated or combined to constitute a coherent whole. We refer to the specific, coherent combination for each period as the "mode of regulation."

ALAIN LIPIETZ

From "Redéploiment et espace économique," *Travaux et recherches de prospectives* (September 1982), no. 85:

A regime of accumulation does not float, disembodied, in the ethereal world of schemas of reproduction. For one or another such schema to be realized and reproduced over a prolonged period, it is necessary for institutional forms, procedures, and habits to act as coercive or inciting forces, leading private agents to conform to the schema. This set of forms is called a "mode of regulation." As we shall see, a regime of accumulation cannot correspond to just any mode of regulation. Economic crises, which appear to be a general, manifest mismatch between supply and demand, may in reality reflect a variety of underlying relationships.

From *Crise et inflation, pourquoi?* (Paris: Maspero, 1979), p. 36:

If the "unity" of the contradiction (here, between the private and social character of production) appears in reproduction, "struggle" appears in the uncertainty of sales, of the realization of commodities. However, "unity" and "struggle" form a contradiction, under the relative domination of unity. How can we think about this unity of "unity" (reproduction) and "struggle" (uncertainty)? In the work that you are about to read, I propose to introduce the concept of regulation.

We will designate the manner in which unity imposes itself through the struggle of the elements of the system as "regulation." This is an enigmatic definition, which cannot be clarified until we look at the specific contradictions involved. However, a word is in order on the distinction between this and other senses of the term.

If regulation essentially designates the relative, temporary primacy of unity over struggle, there is a strong tendency, when discussing regulation, to reestablish the absolute primacy of unity, and, indeed, to eliminate struggle altogether. Such is the origin of the generally accepted understandings of this word. Thus, for instance, Canguilhem offered this widely accepted definition: "Regulation is the adjustment, in conformity with certain rules or norms, of several movements or acts, and their effects or products, which are initially distinct due to their diversity or succession."

FORTUNE DI RUZZA

From "L'idée de régulation en économie politique," in Research Group on the Regulation of Capitalist Economies (GRREC), ed., *Crise et régulation* (Grenoble: Presses Universitaires de Grenoble, 1983), pp. 7–8.

Fundamentally, capitalism is contradictory because it is constituted by contradictions. In this context, regulation is what keeps the system from breaking up because of the centrifugal effects resulting from the contradictions. Consequently, ... the idea of regulation is inseparable from the idea of contradiction. One could ... take this idea further: regulation is the regulation of contradictions by contradictions. In other words, capitalist regulation is a contradictory process of regulation. It combines social practices which are contradictory (not simply incoherent or incompatible) into a single set, and it bears within itself the conditions which give rise to crisis.

The social procedures of regulation are the historical forms of the articulation of competition and the class struggle.

A mode of regulation is a combination of procedures of regulation which are consistent among themselves and with the other characteristic variables of the economic instance (e.g. the regularly changing variables: concentration of capital, the spaces over which firms operate, technological change).

A BRIEF COMMENTARY

The reader may compare these different definitions; I limit myself to listing the broad points of agreement among them:

■ the rejection of the general equilibrium approach;

■ the richness—and poverty—of the concept of reproduction in the Marxist analyses inspired by structuralism;

■ the desire to introduce the element of historical time into the analysis, along with changes in capitalism's social forms and the modalities of dynamic short- and medium-term adjustment; and

■ the intent to combine the theoretical elaboration of intermediate concepts with the periodization of systems of regulation.

But certain differences or disagreements are evident with respect to other problems of theory or method:

■ whether there are laws regarding tendencies (toward falling rates of profit, the equalization of rates of profit, or the concentration of capital);

■ the lesser or greater emphasis placed upon the contradictions within or the temporary coherence of the system of regulation; and

■ implicit positions concerning whether the Marxist theory of value is necessary for the construction of the concepts of accumulation and regulation.

Appendix 2. A Schematic Presentation of the Concepts of Regulation Theory

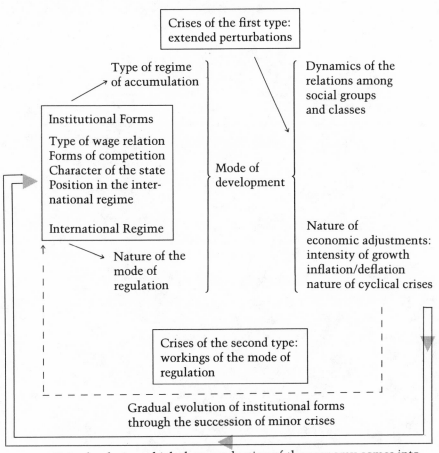

Crises of the first type:
extended perturbations

Type of regime
of accumulation

Dynamics of the
relations among
social groups
and classes

Institutional Forms

Type of wage relation
Forms of competition
Character of the state
Position in the inter-
national regime

Mode of
development

International Regime

Nature of the
mode of
regulation

Nature of
economic adjustments:
intensity of growth
inflation/deflation
nature of cyclical crises

Crises of the second type:
workings of the mode of
regulation

Gradual evolution of institutional forms
through the succession of minor crises

Episodes during which the reproduction of the economy comes into
contradictions with the social forms supporting them: the GREAT
CRISES, or STRUCTURAL CRISES, which fall into two types:

Crises of the third type:
of the mode of regulation

Crises of the fourth type:
of the regime of accumulation
and mode of regulation

Appendix 3. On the Differences Among Regimes of Accumulation

I. THE NEED TO GO BEYOND TRADITIONAL SCHEMAS OF REPRODUCTION

The point of the concept of regimes of accumulation is to make explicit the factors of cohesion which ensure the reproduction of an economic system for a time, until a new blockage or form of structural crisis is encountered. The traditional starting point for Marxist economists has been formalized schemas of reproduction, but often they have come to sharply divergent conclusions. Some choose parameters which allow the reproduction of the system in equilibrium (in particular, without a tendency for the rate of profit to fall), then show that such is possible. Others choose a different set of parameters which lead to the collapse of the system, due, for example to "shrinking" reproduction or explosive fluctuations. The debates on the subject have not produced much clarity, because arithmetical exercises have taken precedence over economic analysis, and even more because the economic behavior predicted depends on the set of parameters assumed.

Researchers using the regulation approach have sought to overcome these difficulties in two ways. To start with, they have attempted to justify by historical and empirical analysis the states that they postulate for the key parameters in the accumulation process. These include the ways in which productivity gains are obtained and their intensity, the lesser or greater capital intensity of production, the division of profit and investment between sectors, and the determinants of demand for consumer products. They have then used those parameters as the bases for different formal models, which are abstract representations of regimes of accumulation observed over the history of the dominant and dominated economies.

Chapter 1 of Aglietta's thesis (1974) is a study of the dynamics of profit rates according to the forms of the mechanization of labor, the manner in which productivity gains are transmitted from sector I (means of production) to sector II (means of consumption), and more generally, whether the extraction of absolute or relative surplus value is dominant. Billaudot, for his part, presented formalizations of the relation between the organic composition of capital in volume and value and the changes in productivity it induces in chapter 2 of his thesis (1976), finding different patterns of evolution depending on changes in capital intensity. In addition, he tested this schema against the evolution of the principal OECD economies. Lorenzi, Pastré, and Toledano made use of Billaudot's analytical framework in their joint work (1980), organizing their analysis of the current crisis around a formalized model of the intensive mode of accumulation, which they contrasted with the extensive mode.

A number of works by Bertrand took this line of inquiry much further, beginning with much more rigorous statistical treatment. He obtained a statistical description of two sectors by inverting an input-output table on the basis of the two components of final demand: consumption and capital formation (1978). He also elaborated theoretical models relating the evolution of the organic composition of capital to the specific productivity, price, and wage dynamics of France's growth mode in the postwar era (1983). In addition, he sketched out a comparison of the development of the crises of 1929 and the present day on the basis of this model (1981).

Finally, other studies have suggested purely theoretical formulations, either in order to connect up with some key models in the literature on growth and business cycles (Boyer 1975), or to examine the potential long-term consequences of various possible regimes of accumulation in the United States and France (Fagerberg 1984). An even more difficult and hardly-explored field is that of the regimes of accumulation in the dominated economies. Their outward-looking orientation and the essential role which non-capitalist relations play within them have called for a novel theoretical approach, of which Garcia Kobek (1982) offers an initial outline.

II. VARIATIONS IN REGIMES OF ACCUMULATION OVER TIME AND SPACE

All this theoretical work would be of little interest if it had produced only one or two models of regimes of accumulation. However, the associated historical studies, conducted principally on France and America, have revealed striking differences in the ways in which the economic circuit is closed in those countries (and by implication, in the other dominant economies as well). These quantitative differences, concerning factors such as growth rates, investment levels, and the breadth of economic fluctuations can be related to different regimes of accumulation.

In order to give the reader a more concrete impression of the results of the above-mentioned work, table 2 summarizes the characteristics of the three principal regimes of accumulation which have appeared over the past 150 years and those of a fourth which has probably arisen since the mid-1960s. They are defined with respect to the five components emphasized by the definition in the text of this book. However, we do not pretend to explain why these regimes function as coherent wholes; interested readers can consult the works cited above.

One might be tempted to apply the same schemas to economies whose industrialization is much more recent, or altogether embryonic, in terms of the well known theory of the stages of economic growth. The first attempts to apply regulation theory to the dominated economies often succumbed to the temptations of such analogies, viewing them as simply lagging behind the older industrial countries. It took a second wave of work before novel analyses appeared, corresponding to the actual histories of countries such as Chile, Venezuela, Mexico, and the Canadian province of Quebec (Ominami 1980; Hausmann 1982; Soria 1984; Letourneau 1984; Garcia Kobek 1982).

We owe the first attempt to set out a synthesis of the various modes of development and nondevelopment of the so-called peripheral or Third World countries to Ominami. Its originality lies precisely in showing that behind these two terms there are a number of sharply contrasting logics. Table 3 summarizes five of the regimes which he described.

TABLE 2. Regimes of Accumulation in the Dominant Economies

	Extensive Accumulation
Production organization	Simple cooperation: Low rate of productivity growth
Time horizon for capital formation	Short, because subject to immediate validation by the market
Income distribution (wages, profits, deductions)	Governed by the short-run phases of the accumulation process
Composition of social demand	Capital formation plays the motor role, final consumption a secondary one
Articulation with other relations of production	Workers reproduced outside of capitalism (petty production, family, etc.)
EXAMPLES	France (first half 19th century)

TABLE 2. (cont.)

Intensive Accumulation without Mass Consumption	Intensive Accumulation with Mass Consumption	Extensive Accumulation with Mass Consumption
Taylorist restructuring of production; big production; big productivity increases	Fordist deepening of mechanism; even higher productivity gains	Exhaustion of Fordism and previous sources of production gains
Slightly longer, due to greater capital intensity	Multi-year, the validation of investments occuring over their expected duration	Shortens, due to economic instability and major uncertainties
Attenuation of wage reductions	Contractualization of direct and indirect wages	Institutionalized division challenged
Consumption diffused more widely, investment remains preponderant	Simultaneous dynamic linking consumption and investment	Previous tendencies and patterns break down
Slow insertion of workers into wage labor, international relations playing a key role	Workers depend on wage labor for reproduction, modification of needs accompanying internationalization	Restructuring of relations with international and domestic economies
U.S., France (between wars)	Europe, U.S. (after 1950)	U.S. (since 1960s)

TABLE 3. Regimes of Accumulation in the Dominated Economies

	Pre-Industrial	*Rentier*
Production organization	Traditional in agriculture, diversified in the export sector	Marginality of industry, Taylorism and Fordism
Time horizon for capital formation	Conditioned by insertion in the international economy; no intersectional coherence of national economy	Long in certain sectors including large projects (oil, industry)
Income distribution (wages, profits, deductions	Opposition between agriculture and rest of the economy	Circulation of rents shapes evolution of other revenue
Composition of social demand	Dichotomy between investment circuit and traditional consumption	Imports close circuits of investment and consumption
Articulation with other relations of production	Capitalist relations of export sector the exception	Rentier relations dominate the logic of capitalism
Examples	Majority of African countries	Saudi Arabia, Venezuela

TABLE 3. (cont.)

Inward-Looking Industrialization	Taylorism	Mixed
Low rate of productivity, growth, extensive accumulation	Taylorist or Fordist thru delocalization of center's labor process	Bases of intensive accumulation, persistence of traditional agriculture
Short/medium term linked to the protection of the domestic market	Rather long-term through strategies of backward linkages	Stabilized by a relatively protected internal market
No link between real wages and productivity	Free management of the labor force, dynamic growth of profit	Profit favored by isolation from international competition
Investment and consumer durables rely on imports	Exports lead demand, esp final consumption	Limitation of durable goods production by income distribution; dependence of investment on external sources
Relations with the peasantry and international markets	Articulation with international economy essential	Possibilities of pre-capitalist agriculture and oil rent
Colombia, Peru	South Korea, Taiwan, Thailand	Brazil, India, Mexico

Selected Bibliography

The Basic Texts

Aglietta, M. 1974. Accumulation et régulation du capitalisme en longue période: Exemple des Etats-Unis, 1870–1970. Doctoral thesis, University of Paris-I.

Aglietta, M. 1976. 1982. 2d ed. *Régulation et crises du capitalisme.* Paris, Calmann-Lévy. English edition: *A Theory of Capitalist Regulation: The American Experience.* London: New Left Books, 1979.

Aglietta, M., and A. Brender. 1984. *Les métamorphoses de la société salariale.* Paris: Calmann-Lévy.

Aglietta, M., and A. Orlean. 1982. *La violence de la monnaie.* Paris: Presses Universitaires de France.

André, C., and R. Delorme. 1983b. *L'Etat de l'économie.* Paris: Seuil.

Benassy, J., R. Boyer, and R. Gelpi. 1979. "Régulation des économies capitalistes et inflation." *Revue Economique,* vol. 30, no. 3.

Bertrand, H. 1978. "Une nouvelle approche de la croissance française de l'après-guerre: l'analyse en sections productives." *Stastiques et Etudes financières,* Orange series, no. 35.

Bertrand, H. 1983. "Accumulation, régulation, crise: un modèle sélectionnel théorique et appliqué." *Revue Economique,* vol. 34, no. 6.

Billaudot, B. 1976. "L'accumulation intensive du capital." Doctoral thesis, University of Paris-I.

Boyer, R. 1979. "La crise actuelle: une mise en perspective historique: Quelques réflections à partir d'une analyse du capitalisme française en longue période." *Critiques de l'économie politique,* no. 7/8, pp. 3–113.

Boyer, R., ed. 1986a. *La flexibilité du travail en Europe.* Paris: La Découverte.

Boyer, R., ed. 1986b. *Capitalismes fin du siècle.* Paris: Presses Universitaires de France.

Boyer, R., and J. Mistral. 1978. 2d ed., 1983. *Accumulation, inflation, crises,* Paris: Presses Universitaires de France.

Canguilhem, G. 1980. "Régulation." *Encyclopedia Universalis,* 14:1.

CEPREMAP-CORDES. (J. Benassy, R. Boyer, R. Gelpi, A. Lipietz, J. Mistral, J. Munoz, and C. Ominami) 1977. *Approches de l'inflation: l'exemple français.* Research contract no. 22, mimeo.

Coriat, B. 1978. *L'atelier et le chronomètre.* Paris: Christian Bourgois.

Destanne de Bernis, G. 1977. "Régulation ou équilibre dans l'analyse économique." In A. Lichnerowicz, ed., *L'Idée de régulation dans les sciences.* Paris: Maloine-Doin.

Destanne de Bernis, G. 1983a. "De quelques questions concernant la théorie des crises." *Cahiers de l'ISMEA,* Series HS, no. 25 *(Economies et sociétés),* pp. 1277–1330.

Destanne de Bernis, G. 1983b. "Une alternative à l'hypothese de l'équilibre économique général: la régulation de l'économie capitaliste." In GRREC 1983, *Crise et régulation.* Grenoble: Presses Universitaires de Grenoble.

GRREC. 1983. *Crise et régulation.* Grenoble: Presses Universitaires de Grenoble.

Lipietz, A. 1979. *Crise et inflation, pourquoi?* Paris: Maspero.

Lipietz, A. 1983. *Le monde enchanté: De la valeur à l'envol inflationniste.* Paris: La Découverte-Maspero; English edition: *The Enchanted World.* London: Verso, 1985.

Lipietz, A. 1984. *L'audace ou l'enlisement.* Paris: La Découverte.

Lipietz, A. 1985. *Mirages et miracles: Problèmes de l'industrialisation dans le tiers monde.* Paris, La Découverte; English edition: *Mirages and Miracles.* London: Verso, 1987.

Lorenzi, J., Pastré, O., and Toledano, J. 1980. *La crise du XXe siècle* (Paris, Editions Economica).

Mazier, J., M. Baslé, and J. Vidal. 1984. *Quand les crises durent . . .* Paris: Editions Economica.

Ominami, C. 1986. *Le Tiers monde dans la crise* (Paris, La Découverte).

Case Studies and Supplementary References

Aglietta, M. 1986. *La fin des devises clés.* Paris: La Découverte.

Aglietta, M., A. Orlean, and G. Oudiz. 1980. "Contraintes de change et régulations macroéconomiques nationales." *Recherches Economiques de Louvain,* 46(3):175–206.

André, C. and R. Delorme. 1983a. "Matériaux pour une comparaison internationale de l'évolution des dépenses publiques en longue période: Le cas de six pays industrialisés." *Statistiques et Etudes financières,* Red Series, no. 390.

Barou, Y. and B. Keizer. 1984. *Les Grandes Economies.* Paris: Seuil.

Bertrand, H. et al. 1981. "Les deux crises des années trente et des années soixante-dix." *Revue Economique.*

Billaudot, B. and A. Gauron. 1985. *Croissance et crise: Vers une nouvelle croissance.* Paris: La Découverte.

Bluestone, B. and Harrison, B. 1987. "The growth of low-wage employment, 1963–1986." Paper presented at the American Economic Association Annual Meeting, Chicago.

Borelly, R. 1975. *Les disparités sectorielles de taux de profit.* Grenoble: Presses Universitaires de Grenoble.

Boyer, R. 1975. "Modalities de la régulation d'économies capitalistes dans la longue période: quelques formalisations simples." Paper, CEPREMAP, Paris.

Boyer, R. 1978. "Les salaires en longue période." *Economie et statistiques,* no. 103, pp. 99–118.

Boyer, R. 1983. "L'Introduction du taylorisme en France à la lumière de recherches récentes: Quels apports et quels enseignements pour le temps présent?" *Travail et emploi,* no. 18, pp. 17–41.

Boyer, R. 1985. "Formes d'organisation implicites à la théorie générale: Une interprétation de l'essor puis de la crise des politiques économiques keynésiennes", in A. Barrère, ed. *Keynes aujourd'hui: théories et politiques* (Paris, Editions Economica), pp. 541–559.

Boyer, R. 1988. "Formalizing With Growth Regimes," in G. Dosi, ed., *Technical Change and Economic Theory*. London: Pinter.

Boyer, R., and B. Coriat. 1986. "Technical Flexibility and Macro-Stabilization. *Richerche Economiche* 40(4):771–835.

Boyer, R. and J. Mistral. 1983. "Le temps présent: La crise: (I) D'une analyse historique à une vue prospective; (II) Pesanteur et potentialités des années quatre-vingt." *Annales (Economies, sociétés, civilisations)*, nos. 3 and 4, pp. 483–506 and 773–789.

Boyer, R. and P. Petit. 1981. "Progrès technique, croissance, et emploi: un modèle d'inspiration kaldorienne pour six industries européennes." *Revue Economique*, 32(6):1113–1153.

Boyer, R. and P. Ralle. 1986. "L'Insertion internationale conditionne-t-elle les formes nationales de l'emploi? Convergences ou différenciations des pays européens." *Economie et société, Cahiers de l'ISMEA*, no. P29.

Capian, A. 1973. "Aspects internationaux de l'accumulation cyclique du capital, 1870–1970." Doctoral dissertation, University of Paris-I.

CEPII. 1983. *Economie Mondiale: la montee des tensions*. Paris: Editions Economica.

CEPII. 1984. *Economie Mondiale 1980–1990: La fracture?* Paris: Editions Economica.

CEPII. 1986. *L'Après-Dollar: Analyse et simulation du système multi-dévises*. Paris: Editions Economica.

Chavance, B. 1984. "Les formes actuelles de crise dans les économies de type soviétique." *Critiques de l'Economie politique*, no. 26–27, pp. 225–245.

Coriat, B. 1982. "Relations industrielles, rapport salarial, et régulation." *Consommation*, no. 3.

Coriat, B. 1985 "L'emploi dans les stratégies négociées d'automatisation: le modèle automobile américain." Paper, CRESST, Paris.

Gelpi, R. 1982. "Mécanismes de la création monétaire et régulations économiques." Doctoral dissertation, University of Paris-IX.

Grando, J., G. Margirier, and B. Ruffieux. 1980. "Rapport salarial et compétitivité des économies nationales: analyse des économies brittanique, italienne, et ouest-allemande depuis 1950. Doctoral thesis, University of Grenoble-II.

Lafont, J., D. LeBorgne, and A. Lipietz. 1980. "Redéploiement industriel et espace économique: une étude intersectorielle comparative." *Travaux et recherches de prospectives* (September 1982), no. 85.

Michalet, C., B. Madeuf, and C. Ominami. 1984. "D'une crise internationale à une crise mondiale." *Critiques de l'Economie Politique*, no. 26–27, pp. 188–209.

Mistral, J. 1981. "La diffusion internationale de l'accumulation intensive et sa crise." In J.-F. Reiffers, ed., *La Recherche en Economie internationale*.

Mistral, J. 1986. "Régime internationale et trajectoires nationales." R. Boyer, ed., *Capitalismes fin de siècle*. pp. 167–202. Paris: Presses Universitaires de France.

Rosenberg, S. 1988. "The Restructuring of the Labor Market, the Labor Force, and the Nature of Employment Relations in the United States." Paper presented at the Conference on Regulation Theory, Barcelona.

Unité de Recherche Grenobloise sur les Economes et les Normes du Socialisme Existante (URGENSE) 1982. "Un taylorisme arythmique dans les économies planifiées du centre." *Critiques de l'Economie politique*, no. 19, pp. 99–146.

Foreign Works Close to the Regulation Approach

Aboites, J. 1986. "Régime d'accumulation, rapport salarial et crises au Mexique, 1940–1982." Mimeo.

Berger, Suzanne B. 1981. *Organizing Interests in Western Europe.* New York: Cambridge University Press.

Bowles, S. 1985. "The Production Process in a Competitive Economy." *American Economic Review*, 75(1):13–36.

Bowles, S. and R. Boyer. 1988. "Labor Discipline and aggregate demand: A Macroeconomic Model." *American Economic Review*, 78(2):395–400.

Bowles, S., D. Gordon and T. Weiskopf. 1983. *Beyond the Waste Land.* New York: Doubleday/Anchor.

Bowles, S., D. Gordon, and T. Weiskopf. 1983. "Long Swings and the Non-Reproductive Cycle." *American Economic Review*, vol. 73, no. 2.

Cassiers, I. 1986. "Croissance, crise, et régulation en économie ouverte: la Belgique entre les deux guerres." Doctoral Thesis, Catholic University of Louvain.

DeVroey, M. 1984. "A Regulation Approach Interpretation of the Contemporary Crisis." *Capital and Class*, no. 23.

Drache, D. and H. Glasbeek. 1988. "The New Fordism in Canada: Capital's offensive, Labor's Opportunity." Paper presented at the Conference on Regulation Theory, Barcelona.

Fagerberg, G. 1984. "The 'Regulation School' and the Classics: Modes of Accumulation and Modes of Regulation in a Classical Model of Economic Growth." *CEPREMAP*, Orange cover, no. 8426.

Garcia-Kobek, A. 1982. "La Notion de régulation: une référence méthodologique pour l'analyse des économies périphériques." D.E.A. thesis, University of Paris-I.

Glyn, A., A. Hughes, A. Lipietz, and A. Singh. 1986. "The Rise and Fall of the Golden Age: An Historical Analysis of Postwar Capitalism in the Developed Market Economies." Mimeo. Macroeconomic Policies Project, World Institute of Development Economics Research, United Nations University, Helsinki.

Guitterez-Garcia, E. 1983. "L'accumulation du capital et le mouvement ouvrier au Mexique: 1950–1960." Doctoral thesis, University of Paris:-VIII.

Haussmann, R. 1981. "State Landed Property Oil Rent and Accumulation in Venezuela: An Analysis in Terms of Social Relations." Ph.D dissertation, Cornell University.

Haussmann, R. and G. Marquez. 1986. "Du bon côté du choc pétrolier." In R. Boyer, ed. *Capitalismes fin de siècle.* Paris: Presses Universitaires de France.

Hillcoat, G. 1976. "La crise des modèles de développement en Amérique Latine: de la substitution d'importations à l'économie tournée vers l'extérieur." Doctoral dissertation, University of Paris.

Hollingsworth, G. 1988. "Comparing Capitalist Economies: Variations in the Governance of Sectors." Paper, University of Wisconsin, Madison.

Juillard, M. 1988. "Un schéma de réproduction pour l'économie des Etats-Unis, 1948–1980: une tentative de modélisation et de quantification." Doctoral thesis, University of Geneva.

Juilliard, M., H. Bertrand, and J. Pisani-Ferry. 1981. "The Departmental Analysis of Growth: A Brief Comparison Between Postwar France and U.S.A." In *Proceedings of the Third Hungarian Conference on Input-Output Techniques, 3–5 November.* Budapest: Statistical Publishing House, 1982.

Karzenstein, P. 1984. *Corporatism and Change.* Ithaca: Cornell University Press.

Keohane, R. 1982. "The Demand for International Regimes." *International Organization,* vol. 36, no. 2.

Lazonick, W. 1986. "Organizations and Markets in Capitalist Development." Mimeo. Macroeconomic Policies Project, World Institute of Development Economics Research, United Nations University, Helsinki.

Letourneau, J. 1984. "Accumulation, régulation, et sécurité du revenué au Québec au début des années soixante." Doctoral thesis, Pierre Laval University, Quebec.

Ominami, C. 1980. "Croissance et stagnation au Chili: éléments pour l'étude de la régulation dans une économie sous-développée." Doctoral Thesis, University of Paris-x.

Perez, C. 1981. "Structural Change and Assimilation of New Technologies in the Economic and Social Systems." *Futures* (October), vol. 15.

Piore, M. and P. Doeringer. 1972. *Internal Labor Markets and Manpower Analysis.* Lexington: Heath.

Piore, M. and C. Sabel. 1984. *The Second Industrial Divide: Possibilities of Prosperity.* New York: Basic Books.

Reich, E., D. Gordon, and R. Edwards. 1982. *Segmented Work, Divided Workers: The Historical Transformation of Labor in the U.S.* New York: Cambridge University Press.

Sabel, C. 1982. *Work and Politics: The Division of Labor in Industry.* New York: Cambridge University Press.

Schmitter, P. and G. Lembruch. 1979. *Trends Toward Corporatist Intermediation.* London: Sage Publications.

Soria, V. 1985. "Formas institucionales, reproducciòn, y regulaciòn economica en la Nueva España, 1521–1570." Mimeo. CEPREMAP, Paris.

Taylor, L. 1983. *Structuralist Macroeconomics: Applicable Models for the Third World.* New York: Basic Books.

Taylor, L. 1986. "Economic Openness: Problems to the Century's End." Mimeo. Macroeconomic Policies Project, World Institute of Development Economics Research, United Nations University, Helsinki.

Velasco e Cruz, G. 1985. "La pertinence des problématiques en termes de régulation pour le Brésil: premiers résultats d'une étude historique." Mimeo. Seminar on the history and theory of economic crises, Ecole des Hautes Etudes en Sciences Sociales, Paris.

Weisskopf, T. 1988. "The Effect of Unemployment on Labor Productivity: An International Comparative Analysis." *International Review of Applied Economics,* 1(2):127–151.

Selected Bibliography

Critiques of the Regulation Approach

Barrère, C., G. Kebabdjian, and O. Weinstein. 1984. "L'accumulation intensive, norme de lecture du capitalisme?" *Revue économique*, no. 3, pp. 479–507.

Bernstein, M. 1988. "The Great Depression and Regulation Theory: A North American perspective." Paper presented at the Conference on Regulation Theory, Barcelona.

Brenner, R. 1988. "The Regulation Approach: A Historical Viewpoint." Paper presented at the Conference on Regulation Theory, Barcelona.

DeBrunhoff, S. 1980. "Sur la notion de régulation." In J. Delaunay, ed., *Acutalité du marxisme*. Paris: Anthropos, 1982.

Delaunay, J. 1985. "Questions posées à la théorie dite de 'la régulation monopoliste.' " *Cahiers de l'ISMEA*, forthcoming.

DeVroey, M. 1982. "Théorie de la régulation et définition de l'inflation. Quelques remarques conceptuelles." Mimeo, Conference on Regulation and Crisis, December 11–12, 1981, University of Paris-I.

Dumenil, G. and D. Levy. 1988. "Theory and Facts: What Can We Learn from a Century of History of the U.S. Economy?" Paper presented at the Conference on Regulation Theory, Barcelona.

Galibert, A. and J. Pisani-Ferry. 1986. "Y a-t-il une école de la régulation." *Alternatives conomiques* (May–June), reprinted in *Problèmes Economiques*, no. 1984.

Kölm, S-.C. 1986. *Philosophie de l'économie*. Paris: Seuil.

Mingat, A., P. Salmon, and A. Wolfesperger. 1985. *Méthodologie Economique*. Paris: Presses Universitaires de France.

Noël, A. 1986. "Accumulation, Regulation, and Social Change: An Essay on French Political Economy." Mimeo, Graduate School of International Studies, University of Denver. *International Organization*, forthcoming.

Noel, A. 1988. "Action collective, partis politiques et relations industrielles: une logique politique sur le thème de la régulation." Paper presented at the Conference on Regulation Theory, Barcelona.

Palloix, C. and P. Zarifian. 1980. *De la socialisation*, Paris: Maspero.

Paveigne, C. 1984. "Les Régulateurs: un réformisme du temps de crise." *La Cause communiste*, no. 8, pp. 35–49.

Peaucelle, I. and P. Petit. 1988. "Croissance économique, profit, et formes de motivations salariales: l'incidence de la protection sociale." Paper presented at the Conference on Regulation Theory, Barcelona.

Rolle, P. 1980. "Le Capitalisme perpétuel." *Enjeu*, no. 11, pp. 20–23.

Steinberg, B. 1986. "Le reaganisme et l'économie américaine dans les années 1980." *Critiques de l'Economie politique*.

Storper, M. and A. Scott. 1988. "The Geographical Foundations and Social Regulation of Flexible Production Complexes." Paper presented at the Conference on Regulation Theory, Barcelona.

Velz, P. 1983. "Fordisme, rapport salarial, et complexité des pratiques sociales." *Critiques de l' conomie politique*, no. 23–24.

Other Works Cited

Akerlof, G. 1984. *An Economic Theorist's Book of Tales*. New York: Cambridge University Press.

Aoki, M. 1984. *The Co-Operative Game Theory of the Firm*. Oxford: Clarendon Press.

Baran, P. and P. Sweezy. 1966. *Monopoly Capital*. Harmondsworth, Penguin.

Benassy, J. 1984. *Macroéconomie et théorie du déséquilibre*. Paris: Dunod.

Berle, A. and G. Means. 1933. *The Modern Corporation and Private Property*. New York: Macmillan.

Burgière, A. 1986. "L'Ecole des *Annales*." In *Dictionnaire des Sciences Historiques*, pp. 46–52. Paris: Presses Universitaires de France.

Chamberlain, E. 1933. *The Theory of Monopolistic Competition*. Cambridge: Harvard University Press.

Davies, R. 1983. "The Comparative Political Economy of Wage Determination: A Quantitative Analysis for the Group of Ten." (Paper presented at the Congress of the International Association for Labor Relations).

Dosi, G., L. Orsenigo, and G. Silverberg. 1986. "Innovation, Diversity, and Diffusion: A Self-Organization Model." (Paper, University of Sussex).

Friedman, M. and A. Schwartz. 1963. *A Monetary History of the United States*. Princeton: Princeton University Press.

Gordon, R. 1984. "Wage-Price Dynamics and the National Rate of Unemployment in Eight Large Industrialized Nations." Paper, OECD Workshop on Price Dynamics and Economic Policy, Paris.

Guttmann, R. 1987. "Changing of the Guard at the Fed." *Challenge* (November–December), pp. 4–9.

Hess, F. 1983. *The Economics of Organization*. Amsterdam: North Holland.

Hounshell, D. A. 1984. *From the American System to Mass Production, 1800–1932: The Development of Manufacturing Technology in the U.S*. Baltimore: Johns Hopkins University Press.

Keynes, J. 1936. *The General Theory of Employment, Interest, and Money*. New York: Harcourt.

Lucas, R. 1984. *Studies in Business Cycle Theory* Cambridge: MIT Press.

Malinvaud, E. 1978. "Nouveaux développements de la théorie macroéconomique du chômage", *Revue Economique*, no. 29, pp. 9–25.

Malinvaud, E. 1983. *Essais sur la théorie du chômage*. Paris: Calmann-Lévy.

Malinvaud, E. 1986. "Les causes de la montée du chômage en France." *Revue Française d'Economie*, 1(1):50–84.

Marglin, S. 1984. *Growth, Distribution, and Prices*. Cambridge: Harvard University Press.

Minsky, H. 1975. *John Maynard Keynes*. New York: Columbia University Press.

Minsky, H. 1982. *Can "It" Happen Again?* New York: Sharpe.

Mitchell, W. 1930. *Business Cycles: The Problem and Its Setting*. New York: National Bureau for Economic Research.

Nelson, R., and S. Winter. 1982. *An Evolutionary Theory of Economic Change*. Cambridge: Harvard University Press.

Piore, M., ed. 1979. *Unemployment and Inflation: Institutionalist and Structuralist Views*. New York: Sharpe.

Robinson, J. 1943. *The Theory of Employment*. Oxford: Blackwell's.

141

Selected Bibliography

Rougerie, R. 1968. "Rémarques sur l'histoire des salaires à Paris." *Le Mouvement Social* (April–June).

Sargent, T. 1979. *Macroeconomic Theory.* New York: Academic Press.

Schor, J. 1985. "Changes in the Cyclical Pattern of Real Wages: Evidence from Nine Countries, 1955–1980." *Economic Journal* (June).

Schotter, A. 1981. *The Economic Theory of Social Institutions.* New York: Cambridge University Press.

Simon, H. 1982. *Models of Bounded Rationality: Behavioral Economics and Business Organization.* Cambridge: MIT Press.

Shaikh, A. 1978. "An Introduction to the History of Crisis Theories." URPE (Union for Radical Political Economics), *U.S. Capitalism in Crisis.* New York: URPE.

Shaikh, A. 1979. "A Marxist Theory of the Business Cycle." *Review of Radical Political Economics* (Spring).

Sweezy, P. 1939. "Demand Under Conditions of Oligopoly." *Journal of Political Economy,* 47:568–573.

Temin, P. 1976. *Did Monetary Forces Cause the Great Depression?* New York: Norton.

Thom, R. 1980. "Halte au hasard, Silence au bruit." *Le Débat* (July–August).

Thurow, L. 1980. *The Zero-Sum Society.* New York: Basic Books.

Williamson, O. 1975. *Markets and Hierarchies: Analysis and Antitrust Implications.* London: Macmillan.

Williamson, O. 1985. *The Economic Institutions of Capitalism.* London: Macmillan.

Index

Aboites, J., 100
Accumulation, regime of: based on mass consumption, 15, 18, 58, 68, 76; capitalist mode of production and, 34-35; commodity relations and, 34-35; crises of mode of development and, 56-58; destabilization of, 103; disequilibrium and, 36, 48; diversity of, 127-29; in dominant economies, 128-133; economic crises and, 34-35; forms of competition and, 39; institutional forms stabilizing, 107-11; international sphere, 17, 89; limits of, 71, 74-75, 82; regulation mode and, 19, 43-44; social conflicts and, 48; state forms and, 42; structural crises and, 51-53, 56-58, 64-65
Aglietta, Michel, 17-18, 23, 73, 78, 81, 94, 107, 117, 127
Agricultural crises, 50
Akerlof, G., 46
Althusserian school, 32-33
American institutionalist school, 64
André, C., 41
Anglo-Saxon corporatist school, 69
Annales school, 21, 29, 30, 70-71
Auto industry, 87

Belgium, 100
Benassy, Jean-Pascal, 8, 88, 118
Bertrand, H., 18, 68, 102, 104, 128
Billaudot, B., 18, 103, 128
Bowles, S., 102
Boyer, Robert, 21, 24, 68, 88, 119-121

Braudel, Fernand, 31, 34
Brazil, peripheral Fordism and, 99-100
Brender, A., 23
Business cycles, 13, 27, 50-51

Canguilhem, G., 15-16, 47
Capital: internationalization of, 74; organic composition of, 128; technical composition of, 102-3; valorization of, 35, 65
Capitalism: accumulation regime and, 34-36; commodity relations and, 33-34; contradictory nature of, 59; cyclical crises and, 50-52; dynamics of, 91, 104-5; economic crises and, 34-35, 49-50; exogenous crises and, 49-50; final crisis in, 58-60; forms of competition and, 39; globalization of, 41; individual vs. collective interests and, 86; industrial, 34, 74; institutional forms and, 37-42; long-run tendencies, 48; loss of hegemony, 89; Marxism and, 12; production relations and, 26, 33, 35, 38; qualitative changes in, 74; social forms and, 33; stagnation in, 27; state forms and, 41-42, 92
Case study, 109
Cassiers, I., 100
Catastrophy theory, 21
Center for International Forecasting and Information (CEPII), 73
Center for Mathematical Economic Forecasting Studies Applied to Planning (CEPREMAP), 18, 78

143

Imperfect competition, 53
Income: distribution of, 50; rights to, 55
Industrial urban lifestyle, 55
Industry: aging of basic, 54; reorganization of, 2
Inflation, 18; credit expansion and, 72; current economic crisis and, 55; debt economies and, 10; disequilibrium theory and, 9; interest rates and, 73; mode of regulation and, 69-70; monetary policies and, 2, 38, 72; origins of, 64; regulation theory and, 72-73; rising rates of, 1; unemployment and, 70
Institutional forms: capitalism and, 37-42; centrality of, 114; competition and, 39; differentiation of, 98-99; dominant mode of production and, 37; economic stability and, 47-48; effectiveness of state interventions and, 75; full employment and, 14; great crises and, 107-11; historical analysis of, 61-62; historically determined, 108-9; innovations in, 112-14; limits of, 56-60; logic of, 62-63, 104-7; mode of development and, 68; mode of regulation and, 43-45; monetary constraint and, 37-38; national, 41; operation of, 44-45; periodization and, 61-62, 68-69; priniciples of, 45, 47; regulation theory and, 22, 80; social relations and, 17, 37-42; state forms and, 41-42; transformations of, 81-82; wage relations and, 38-39, 88
Institutionalism, 24, 64, 78
Institutionalist-historicist school, 80-84
Interest rates: inflation and, 2, 73; international monetary system and, 72; investment decisions and, 10; rising real, 73
International economy: crisis of 1929 and, 54; crisis of regulation in, 55; dollar's stability and, 4, 55; monetary relations, 38
International markets, 17, 27-28

International payments, recession and, 2
Investment, 45; declining industrial, 2; institutional structure and, 107; interest rates and, 10; post-Keynesians and, 10; profitability and, 3, 10
Italy, Fordism in, 80

Juglar cycle, 57

Kaleckian macroeconomics, 14
Keohane, R., 73
Keynes, J., 3, 8, 10-11
Keynesian theory, 1, 55; crisis of 1929 and, 54; current economic crisis and, 92-93; economic instability and, 10-11; Fordism and, 76; generality of, 79; institutionalism and, 69; reflation and, 2; regulation and, 20, 21; resolution of crises and, 109-10; unemployment and, 5, 8, 9; wage determination and, 106
Kolm, S. C., 89
Kondratiev wave, 57, 71
Kuhn, Thomas, 19

Labor, 6-8; accumulated knowledge of, 7; capital relations, 13; contracts and, 46; deepening division of, 36; dual markets and, 22; value of, 17; *see also* Employment; Wage relations
Labrousse, Ernest, 21, 33, 59, 70
Laffer, Arthur, 3
Laws: purpose of, 44; transmutation from individual to collective, 45
Lipietz, Alain, 23, 121-22
Lorenzi, J., 19, 68, 128
Lucas, R., 5

Macroeconomic theories: disequilibrium and, 10-11; microeconomic foundations of, 32; partial regulation and, 63-64; regulation approach and, 14-15, 79; underdeveloped economies and, 65; unorthodox standard model, 101
Malinvaud, E., 9

Social relations: adaptability of, 48;
collapse of, 58-60; determination by
productive forces, 57; economic organization and, 32; historical analysis of, 61-62; institutional forms
and, 17, 37-42, 43; macroeconomic
model, 65; Marxism and, 11-12;
monetary form and, 37; modes of
production and, 32; overall logic of,
32; plasticity in, 58; regulation theory and, 13, 32-34, 85; rules and, 44-
45; stable configurations of, 43
Social sciences, regulation and, 47,
70
Sociopolitical struggles, structural
crises and, 52
Spain, tardy Fordism in, 80
Speculative bubbles, 49
Stagflation, 72
Stagnation, 27, 51, 73, 95
State intervention: active, 20; commodity relations and, 105; compromises and, 47-48; effectiveness of,
75; forms of, 42; functionalist view
of, 47-48; protectionism, 2, 24; socialism and, 93; support for market
and, 93-94
State monopoly capitalism, 16, 92-94,
105
Structural crises, 82; accumulation regime and, 51-53, 56-58, 64-65; economic growth and, 92; of economic
policy, 76-77; origins of, 89; properties of, 91-92; regulation mode and,
51-53, 56-58
Structural forms, *see* Institutional
forms
Supply: Keynesian theory and, 5; supply-side school, 3
Surplus, shrinkage of, 59
Systems engineer, 47
Systems theory, 15, 20

Taxes: emergence of state and, 41; reduced tax base and, 76; regulation
theory and, 24; supply-side theory
and, 3
Taylorism, 39; alternatives to, 74-75;
crisis of 1929 and, 54; structural

crises and, 65; work organization
and, 90
Technology: current economic crisis
and, 89-90; employment effects of,
64; evolutionary model, 101; institutional change and, 57; investment
levels and, 2; potential impact of,
114; productivity and, 95
Thom, R., 77
Toledano, J., 19, 69, 128
Trade: current economic crisis and,
55; protectionism and, 2, 24; regulation theory and, 24; U.S. deficits, 4
Treaty of Versailles, 54
Trotskyites, 92

Underdeveloped economies, macroeconomic theory and, 65
Underemployment, equilibrium of, 8,
13
Unemployment, 2; classical, 8, 9; increasing, 6-8; inflation and, 70;
Keynesian model and, 5-6; long-
term, 7; Marxism and, 8, 9; microeconomic explanations, 5; natural, 6;
post-Keynesian theories and, 11;
structural, 6-8; technological
changes and, 95; temporary, 7; voluntary, 6; *see also* Employment
United States: capital inflows, 4; crisis
in, 104; deregulation and, 3; economic circuit, 129; phase of decline,
112; trade deficit, 4; wage relation
configuration and, 38-39; *see also*
Capitalism

Value, distribution of, 35
Value systems: general equilibrium
theory and, 46; regulating behavior
and, 45
Velasco e Cruz, G., 100
Venezuela, 100
Vidal, J., 23

Wage determination: collective bargaining and, 18, 106; competitive arrangements for, 23; demand and, 86-
87; industrywide diffusion, 86-88;
inflexibility of nominal wages and,

Wage determination (*Continued*)
6-7; institutional changes and, 88;
management objectives and, 7;
mechanisms for, 62-63; monopolistic regulation and, 88; reflation and,
94-95; *see also* Wage relations

Wage relations: capitalist, 33-34 commodity relations and, 6-7, 106; competitive, 39; crisis of 1929 and, 53-
54; demand and, 86-87, 106; differences between nations, 69; economic crises and, 50; Fordism and,
54-55, 73-74; implicit contracts and,
108; institutional forms and, 38-39,
88; modeling regulation modes and,
101; neoclassical approaches, 80; oligopolistic theory and, 9; productivity and, 7, 9, 90; public spending
and, 42; pure commodity exchange
and, 106; regulation school and, 74;
social progress and, 95; *See also* Employment; Labor

Walrasian theory, 8, 79, 81, 86
Weisskopf, T., 102
West Germany, Fordism and, 80
Wolfesperger, A., 78, 80, 87, 91, 94

Zero-sum game, 55